THE
PEOPLE'S
BOOKS

WILD FLOWERS

WILD FLOWERS

BY

MACGREGOR SKENE, D.Sc.

LECTURER ON VEGETABLE PHYSIOLOGY,
ABERDEEN UNIVERSITY

REVISED EDITION

London and Edinburgh:

T. C. & E. C. JACK, LTD. | T. NELSON & SONS, LTD.

1919

CONTENTS.

Introduction. 7

White Flowers 15

Yellow Flowers. 40

Rose Flowers 65

Red Flowers 74

Pale Purple Flowers 77

Purple Flowers 86

Blue Flowers 99

Brown Flowers 106

Green Flowers 110

Flowers rarely found or very Inconspicuous 116

Index of Latin Names 119

Index of English Names. 122

WILD FLOWERS.

INTRODUCTION.

THAT curious characteristic of the human mind
which will scarcely let us rest content in the beauty
of an object, but forces us to seek out the some-
thing concrete with which the beauty is associated,
cannot be better exemplified than by the universal
desire to put a label on the object of our admiration,
be it picture, or mountain, or tree. For most of us
the interest of wild flowers lies chiefly in their æsthetic
appeal; and yet, though it does not affect the love-
liness of the plant, there are few who do not feel their
interest quickened by the knowledge of what the
flower is called. To enable the great majority of
flower-lovers, which has no acquaintance with the
technicalities of botany, to acquire that knowledge
is the aim of this book. In such short space little
more is possible; but the attempt has been made to
indicate in some cases the peculiar interest that a
plant may have for mankind, in others some point
worthy of remark in its own life. The reader will
also observe that plants do not grow at random in
any sort of situation, but that they occur in nature
in definite communities, one set preferring the river-
side, another the woodland, a third the moor or the
pasture. Such indications, though quite inadequate,
may be sufficient to widen somewhat the interest of
our flowers.

The number of technical terms has been reduced to a minimum, hardly a score of words not in everyday use being employed : the meaning of these will be clear to anyone who has read the following introductory paragraphs.

General Structure of the Plant.

Flowering plants are composed of four distinct sets of organs, to each of which is assigned a particular rôle in the life of the whole. (1) The *Root* serves to fix the plant firmly in the soil, and to absorb from the soil the water and the mineral salts which the plant requires. (2) The *Stem* bears the leaves and flowers, holds them in advantageous positions, and carries to them water and various nutrient material. (3) The *Leaves* receive from the root water and mineral substances, and from the air the important gas *carbon dioxide;* from these they are able to build up the food of the plant—such substances as sugar and starch. This they do by virtue of their green colouring-matter, which absorbs a large quantity of light, necessary for the carrying on of the chemical processes involved in the formation of the food substances. (4) The *Flowers* have as their special function the reproduction of the plant by means of seed-formation. In reality the flower is a collection of leaves, deeply modified to enable them to perform their new work ; some produce the true reproductive bodies—the *pollen-grains* and the *ovules*—others protect these, and aid them in various ways.

For our present purpose it is necessary to consider the external form only of these different parts : a fuller treatment of their structure, and of the way in which they carry on their work, is to be found in another of the books of this series, Dr. Marie Stopes' *Modern Botany*.

1. The Root.—Only in comparatively few cases does the root present features of value for the identification of a plant ; of interest are those roots which serve to store food, and so become swollen and *tuberous* (*e.g.* orchis).

2. The Stem.—It may be necessary to note whether the stem is *branched* or without branches—*simple*. Many stems stand straight up—*erect ;* but frequently we meet with plants the stems of which lie along the ground—*prostrate ;* in yet other cases the stem may support itself on external objects—*climb* or *ramble*.

3. The Leaf is typically divided into two parts, the *leaf-stalk* and the *blade ;* very often, however, there is no stalk, and then the leaf is said to be *sessile*. The margin of the blade is sometimes quite smooth—*entire*—but usually it is cut into or notched in various ways. If it presents a series of little teeth pointing forwards, like those of a saw, it is *serrate ;* if the teeth are more irregular and point outwards, it is *toothed*. Often the cutting is much more profound ; it may go right down to the central vein (*mid-rib*) of the leaf, so dividing it into a number of smaller *leaflets*, in which case we have a *compound leaf*, as opposed to a *simple leaf*—one in which the cutting does not reach the mid-rib. If the cutting, though not deep enough to form a compound leaf, yet divides it very deeply, we have a *segmented* leaf ; if the cutting is less marked still, the leaf is said to be *lobed*. In compound, segmented, and lobed leaves the cutting may take place in two different ways : (1) if the leaflets, segments, or lobes radiate out from one point at the apex of the leaf-stalk, the leaf is *palm-compound* (*segmented*, &c.) ; (2) if, on the contrary, they arise at the sides of the mid-rib, it is *feather-compound,* &c. Often the leaflets of a compound leaf are themselves compound, in which case the leaf is *doubly compound :* further complications are adequately described by combinations of the terms given above.

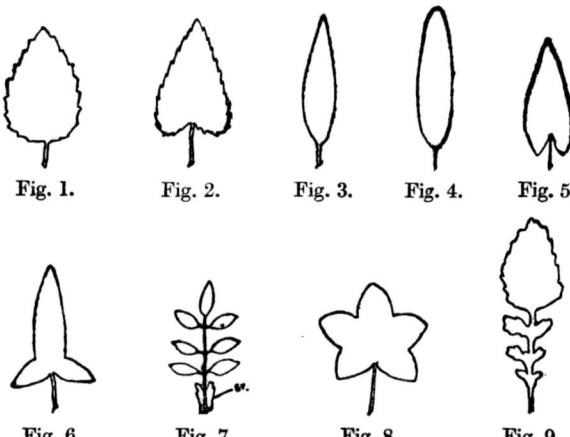

Fig. 1.   Fig. 2.   Fig. 3.   Fig. 4.   Fig. 5.

Fig. 6.   Fig. 7.   Fig. 8.   Fig. 9.

Fig. 1.—Ovate leaf with toothed margins. Fig. 2.—Heart-shaped leaf with serrate margins. Fig. 3.—Lance-shaped leaf. Fig. 4.—Elliptical leaf. Fig. 5.—Arrow-shaped leaf. Fig. 6.—Halbert-shaped leaf. Fig. 7.—Feather-compound leaf with seven leaflets and two stipules (st.). Fig. 8.—Palm-lobed leaf. Fig. 9.—Feather-segmented leaf, lyre-shaped, with coarsely toothed margins.

The actual shape of the leaf or leaflets is described by a series of terms, some of which are self-explanatory, while the meaning of the others may be best understood by reference to the accompanying diagrams. One term requires special mention : by *lyre-shaped* we mean a feather-compound or feather-lobed leaf, in which the terminal lobe or leaflet is larger than the others.

In many plants there are to be found, at the base of the leaf-stalk, two leafy outgrowths, sometimes quite small, sometimes as large as the leaf itself— these are called *stipules*.

Of the *surface* of the leaf, we note that it may be *smooth* or *hairy ;* and of its *texture* that, in a few cases, it is *fleshy* or *leathery*.

4. The Flower.—If we pull the flower of a butter-cup to pieces, we find that it consists of four different kinds of organs. To the outside there is a *whorl* (or circle) of five greenish scales : these are *sepals*, and together make up the *calyx*, which in the bud protects the delicate internal parts of the flower. Then comes a whorl of yellow *petals*, forming the *corolla :* its bright colour, and the fact that frequently, as in this case, there is to be found honey about its base, induce insects to visit the flower. Inside the corolla there is a large number of *stamens ;* each of these consists of a delicate stalk, and a little head, in which is produced the dust-like *pollen*. Finally, in the centre is a number of green grains, the *seed-vessels :* at the tip of the seed-vessel is a receptive spot—the *stigma*—which is frequently borne on a slender stalk—the *style*. Before the flower can set seed, it is necessary for the *ovules*, which are contained in the seed-vessel, to be fertilised, and this can take place only if pollen from the stamens reaches the stigma—the receptive spot of the seed-vessel. It has been found that better and more abundant seed is set if the pollen be obtained from the flower of another plant, and it is for the purpose of attaining this end that the plant invites the visits of insects. These, in their hunt for honey, brush against the stamens and stigma, and as they always carry about a dust of foreign pollen, there is a considerable chance that the stigma of a flower will receive pollen from one of its kind, growing on a separate plant.

The different parts of the flower may be arranged in different ways : frequently a complete set of parts is wanting—the wood anemone, for example, has no corolla, but only a calyx, which has become brightly coloured to take the place of the missing petals. If either stamens, or seed-vessel, be absent, then two kinds of flowers, one male with stamens, one female with seed-vessels, are found, and sometimes on different plants. The numbers of the parts vary greatly. Frequently the parts of a whorl are united to form a single piece. The seed-vessel is often embedded in the flower-stalk, *below* the other parts, instead of being *above* them, as in the buttercup.

The flowers may occur singly in the *axils* of the leaves—that is, in the angle between the leaf and the stem ; but more frequently they are grouped in characteristic *inflorescences*. By a *spike* we mean, in this book, any elongated mass of flowers occupying the apex of a stem or branch. By an *umbel* we mean an inflorescence in which the stem or branch ends abruptly, giving rise to a large number of flower-stalks, the lengths of which are such that the flowers all occupy one level, and so form a flat, pancake-like, or convex, umbrella-like group (*e.g.* Figs. 6, 7). By a *composite head* we mean a close head of flowers surrounded by a number of greenish scales or leaves—the daisy shows this type. If we examine the so-called flower of the daisy, we find that it is made up of a great number of little flowers—those to the centre with a tubular, yellow corolla, stamens, and a seed-vessel ; those to the margin with a white, strap-shaped corolla, and a seed-vessel : while outside is a large number of green scales ; these serve to distinguish this type from the *simple* head of a clover, which does not possess them. The centre part of the daisy flower-head is spoken of as the *disc*, the marginal part as the *ray*.

IDENTIFICATION OF A WILD FLOWER.

Plants are grouped in families, in such a way as to bring together those which show a natural relationship to each other. As the characters on which this *natural* grouping rests are frequently obscure, it has been thought best to employ in this book an *artificial* arrangement, designed to enable the beginner to identify a strange plant by means of its more obvious characters. In the first place the plants dealt with are arranged in *ten colour groups*. As considerable variation occurs in colour, and as the value placed by different people on a particular colour shade is not always the same, it would be well, if, for example, a purplish flower could not be found under *purple*, to try under *pale purple*.

As some of the groups are rather large, it has been found necessary to subdivide them. The method of working the classification employed may best be understood if we take a concrete example. Suppose we have found a specimen of the Greater Stitchwort. It is a white flower, so we turn to the table at the beginning of " White Flowers," and find that these are arranged in three groups. As the Stitchwort has neither composite-heads nor umbels, it must belong to group III. ; here there are two subgroups, in the second of which, *B*, it must be placed, as its leaves are quite simple : we then count the number of stamens, which we find to be ten, and so learn that it is among plants 55–65. It only remains for us to read over the descriptions of these, and to compare our plant with the illustrations, to determine which fits it properly, and so find its name to be *Stellaria Holostea*, the *Greater Stitchwort*.

With the aid of this book it will be found possible to identify a considerable number of our commoner or more striking wild plants; but only about one-sixth of the total number of British species is mentioned. If the interest of the reader carries him beyond the limits of these pages, and is sufficient to nerve him to face the difficulties of a more minute examination, and of a more extended technical vocabulary, we may conclude by advising him to turn his attention to one of the standard works on the subject. Of these two may be mentioned :—Babington's *Manual of British Botany*, 9th ed., and Bentham and Hooker's *Handbook of the British Flora*, 8th ed. As neither is illustrated, we might add, as a companion volume, Smith's *Illustrations of the British Flora*, 6th ed.

For general works on other branches of botany the list of books given in Dr. Marie Stopes' *Modern Botany* should be consulted.

WHITE FLOWERS,
1–50.

I. Flowers grouped in Composite Heads . . . 1–5
II. Flowers grouped in Umbels 6–15
III. Flowers grouped otherwise, or occurring singly 16–50

    A. Leaves compound, deeply cut, or lobed . 16–25
    B. Leaves quite simple, at most toothed . . 26–50

        a. Stamens absent 50
        b. Stamens 2–4 in number . . . 26–32
        c. Stamens 5–7 in number . 33–43, 45, 48
        d. Stamens 8 or more in number . . 44–50

1. Daisy, *Bellis perennis*, Daisy family. The short horizontal underground stem bears rosettes of leaves, which are oval in shape, tapering to the base, and irregularly toothed : from among these arise several flower - stalks, each a few inches high and with a single flower-head : the disc is yellow, the ray white with pink tips : perhaps the commonest of our wild flowers, to be seen during the greater part of the year in grassy places : the flower-heads are very sensitive, closing in darkness and wet weather.

1. Common Daisy.

2. Millefoil, Yarrow, *Achillea Millefolium*, Daisy family. A common and very pretty plant of meadows and pastures : the leaves are 3 to 4 ins. long

15

and lance-shaped in outline, but they are deeply
lobed, and the lobes are cut into fine segments, so
that the leaf has a dainty feather-like appearance :
the stem is about 1 ft. high, and bears a flat head of
small flower-heads : flowers in summer.

3. Sneezewort, *Achillea Ptarmica,* Daisy family.
Like the preceding species, this is one of our common
summer meadow plants : the flower-heads are some-

2. Millefoil.   3. Sneezewort.

what larger but are gathered into the same flat
inflorescence : the stem is 1 to 2 ft. high, and bears
narrow lance-shaped leaves, with serrate margins,
and a shiny surface.

4. Ox-eye, *Chrysanthemum Leucanthemum,* Daisy
family. In hay-fields in summer the large flower-
heads of the Ox-eye, with the broad white rays and
yellow discs, are frequently abundant : the stem is
1 to 2 ft. high and bears only a few flower-heads : the
leaves are dark green, glossy, serrate, and narrow
(2,050)

towards the base. The *Feverfew*, a related species with numerous smaller heads, and compound leaves having lobed ovate leaflets, is found on waste ground.

5. Mayweed, *Matricaria inodora,* Daisy family. A common weed in fields and waste places, flowering in late summer and autumn : the stem is about 1 ft. high and may be branched : the leaves are twice cut and the segments are very narrow, almost hair-like :

| 4. Ox-eye. | 5. Mayweed. |

the flower-heads are few in number, fairly large, with white ray and yellow disc : the plant has a scent resembling, but not so strong as, that of the related *Chamomile.*

6. Hemlock, *Conium maculatum,* Hemlock family. A plant of hedgerows and waste places : it is easily recognised by the fact that the stem (3 to 5 ft. high) is spotted with dull purple, and by its mouse-like smell : the whole plant is smooth, with a slight bloom : the leaves are large and doubly feather-compound :

the secondary leaflets are deeply notched : the large
white umbels are to be seen in summer : the plant
is highly poisonous.

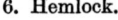

6. Hemlock.　　　　　7. Gout-weed.

7. Gout-weed, Bishop's-weed, *Ægopodium poda-*
graria, Hemlock family.　The leaves of this plant
often cover considerable areas in damp shady places,
and it is frequently an annoying garden weed : the
leaves are large and divided into three leaflets, each
of which is again divided into three leaflets, these
being ovate, serrate, and glossy-green : from among
the leaves rises the flower stem, about 1 to 2 ft. high,
with several smallish umbels of yellowish-white
flowers : flowers in summer.

8. Burnet-Saxifrage, *Pimpinella Saxifraga,* Hemlock family.　A common plant of pasture-land,
flowering in autumn : from the base of the stem
spring a few feather-compound leaves, with ovate,
notched leaflets : the stem (1 to 2 ft. high) looks

bare, as its few leaves are divided into narrow, notched segments : the stem bears several small umbels, which are white or tinged with red.

9. Pig - nut, *Conopodium denudatum,* Hemlock family. The root is a single tuber which lies about 6 ins. underground, and is frequently dug up and eaten by children : the stem is slender, especially below, and about 1 ft. high, with a few rather small umbels : the leaves are doubly feather-compound, and the leaflets deeply notched, giving the plant a very graceful appearance : flowers in early summer.

10. Sweet Cicely, *Myrrhis Odorata,* Hemlock family. The *Myrrh* of country children is fairly common on pastures and damp waste ground : it is a tall (3 ft.) handsome plant with large doubly or

8. Burnet-Saxifrage.   9. Pig-nut.

triply feather-compound leaves : the whole plant is soft with fine hairs : the umbels are large and cream-coloured : the fruits, as well as the leaves and stem, are aromatic and are eaten by children because of their pleasant flavour : flowers in early summer.

11. Shepherd's Needle, *Scandix Pecten-Veneris*, Hemlock family. The English name of this plant of the fields refers to the long (2 ins.) slender needle-like fruits, which are very striking after the flower has fallen : the stem is under 1 ft. high with long

10. Sweet Cicely.   11. Shepherd's Needle.

triply feather-compound, light green leaves, the segments of which are very narrow : the small umbels occur one or two together : flowers summer.

12. Wild Chervil, *Anthriscus sylvestris*, Hemlock family. One of our commonest hedgerow plants : it is coarse, with a rough, furrowed stem about 3 ft. high, and large, doubly feather-compound leaves, the leaflets of which are much notched : the umbels are large, and show well the special advantage of this type of inflorescence—the individual flowers are small and inconspicuous, but in the mass they form a very showy object : the effect is still further enhanced by the fact that the external petals of the external flowers are much enlarged : flowers in spring and early summer. The *Rough Chervil* has less cut leaves and ribbed, instead of smooth, fruits.

13. **Angelica,** *Angelica sylvestris,* Hemlock family. A common plant in damp shady places : the stem

12. Wild Chervil.   13. Angelica.

is smooth, tinged with purple, about 3 ft. high, and bears the large pinkish-white umbels and the leaves : these are large, smooth, doubly compound, with ovate, serrate leaflets : flowers in late summer. A related species cultivated in gardens and occasionally escaping was formerly used in medicine and is still employed in making confectionery.

14. **Cow - parsnip, Hog - weed,** *Heracleum Sphondylium,* Hemlock family. This coarse plant is a common weed of banks and pastures : the stem is

about 4 ft. high, and, as well as the leaves, is rough
with coarse hairs : the leaves are very large and compound, the leaflets being deeply cut into serrate lobes :
the umbels are large, creamy or tinged with red, and
flower about mid-summer.

15. **Hedge Parsley,** *Caucalis Anthriscus,* Hemlock family. The slender stems are usually about
2 ft. high, and carry numerous small umbels of white

14. Cow-parsnip.   15. Hedge Parsley.

or reddish flowers, opening in summer : the fruits
are markedly prickly : the leaves are fine, doubly
feather-compound, and with ovate, serrate leaflets :
the plant is common on banks and in hedges.

16. **Traveller's Joy, Old Man's Beard,** *Clematis Vitalba,* Crowfoot family. One of the most
familiar and beautiful denizens of the English
hedgerows : the stem rambles over bushes and trees,
often almost hiding the hedge : the leaves are
opposite, feather-compound with ovate, coarsely

serrate leaflets : the leaf-stalk acts as a tendril, twisting round any convenient support, and so aiding the plant to climb : the flowers, which appear in

16. Traveller's Joy.   17. Wood Anemone.

June, in small bunches, in the leaf axils, are devoid of petals, and possess only 4 oval greyish sepals : in autumn the flowers are succeeded by clusters of little

18. Water Crowfoot.   19. White Climbing Fumitory.

seed-like fruits, each with a long feathery style, and to these the plant owes its chief claim to beauty.

17. Wood Anemone, *Anemone nemorosa,* Crowfoot family. A familiar plant in shady woods, flowering in spring : the stem is subterranean, and gives rise each year to 2 or 3 leaves, and a slender flower-stalk, which bears 3 leaves and a single flower : the leaves are deeply palm-divided into 3 to 5 notched segments : the flower is devoid of corolla, but the sepals are petal-like, generally white, but sometimes purple in colour.

18. **Water Crowfoot**, *Ranunculus aquatilis*, Crowfoot family. A large number of forms of *Water Crowfoot*, all resembling each other fairly closely, are to

20. Water-Cress.   21. Hairy Bitter-Cress.

be found in our streams and ponds : all have submerged leaves, which are cut into a number of very fine hair-like segments ; some have in addition less divided aërial leaves : the small flowers are produced above the surface of the water ; the petals are white, except for a yellow spot on the inner side : flowers in summer. The *Ivy-leaved Crowfoot* is a form common in ditches, with leaves like those of the ivy.

19. **White Climbing Fumitory**, *Corydalis claviculata*, Fumitory family. A slender rambler, often

attaining a length of 3 to 4 ft., and growing through
and over bushes (especially whin and bramble) : the
leaves are bright green and feather-compound, each
leaflet being divided into three secondary leaflets ;
the tip of the leaf is occupied by the delicate branched
tendril, which enables the plant to climb : the flowers,
which are small and cream-coloured, have a blunt
spur projecting back, and occur in little groups of
four or five in summer.

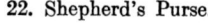

22. Shepherd's Purse.   23. Wood Sorrel.

20. Water-Cress, *Nasturtium officinale*, Cress
family. The *Water-Cress* is found everywhere in
small streams of running water : the stem is usually
1 to 2 ft. long, rising out of the water at least at the
tip, which bears a spike of small white flowers : the
leaves are feather-compound, with ovate leaflets :
the plant is much more slender if it grows out of
water, but in suitable wet positions may be very
luxuriant : flowers in summer.

21. Hairy Bitter-Cress, *Cardamine hirsuta*, Cress
family. A common plant of moist meadows : it has

a rosette of feather-compound leaves, with roundish, toothed leaflets : from this rises the stem about 1 ft. high, with a few leaves and a spike of small white flowers : the hairy sepals distinguish it readily from land forms of the preceding species : flowers from spring to autumn.   The *Common Bitter-Cress* is a larger species with large white flowers, which have conspicuous violet stamens.

22. Shepherd's Purse, *Capsella Bursa - pastoris*, Cress family. Perhaps the commonest of our weeds, found in fields, gardens, roadsides, and woods, flowering almost all the year round : from the rosette of more or less deeply feather-cut leaves springs a stalk about 1 ft. high, with a spike of inconspicuous white flowers : the plant is most readily recognised by its fruits, which are little heart-shaped pouches with the notch turned outwards.

24. Dutch Clover.

23. Wood Sorrel, *Oxalis Acetosella*, Wood Sorrel family.   One of the prettiest of our woodland plants : there is a knotty underground stem, from the apex of which arise the slender leaf-stalks, each with a leaf composed of three heart-shaped leaflets, the base of the heart being turned away from the stalk : among the leaves there appear in early summer one or two flower-stalks, each with a delicate, drooping, bell-like flower, the white petals of which are veined with purple : the leaves, which are occasionally used as a salad, have a pleasant acid flavour.

24. Dutch Clover, *Trifolium repens*, Vetch family.
The stem is more or less prostrate, and gives off leaves
on long stalks ; these are divided into three serrate

25. Meadow-Sweet.   26. Great Bed-straw.

leaflets, and possess ovate stipules ; the flower-stalks
are longer than the leaves, in the axils of which they
grow, and bear heads of cream-coloured flowers,
which turn brown with age : the flowers have a fine
aroma, and are much visited by bees for their honey :
common in pastures and meadows, flowering throughout summer and autumn.

25. Meadow-Sweet, *Spiræa Ulmaria*, Rose
family. The " *Queen-of-the-Meadow* " is frequent
in meadows and on river-banks : the tall (2 to 3 ft.)
stem bears handsome spikes, composed of many
cream-coloured flowers, and large feather-compound
leaves, with alternate pairs of large and small, serrate leaflets : stem and leaves alike have a reddish
tinge : flowers throughout summer : very fragrant.

26. Great Bed-straw, *Galium Mollugo*, Bed-straw family. The stem is long, branched, and scrambling amongst grass and bushes : it bears small, narrow leaves in whorls of 6 to 8 : the small white flowers are grouped in a large, loose, much-branched terminal brush : flowers in late summer.

27. Stone Bed-straw, *Galium Saxatile*, Bed-straw family. A small plant creeping amongst rocks and on short turf : the stem is branched, and has whorls of about 6 small, sharply-pointed leaves : the small white flowers are grouped in loose, branched clusters at the ends of the flowering stems : flowers in late summer.

28. Goose-grass, Cleavers, *Galium Aparine*, Bed-straw family. The long weak stems scramble in

27. Stone Bed-straw.   28. Goose-grass.

thickets : they bear whorls of 6 to 8 leaves, in the axils of which may grow little clusters of small, yellowish-white flowers : the whole plant, especially the fruits, is clad with hooked bristles : these enable the plant to scramble the more securely, and the fruits to hang on to passing animals, and so become dispersed : flowers in summer.

29. **Woodruff,** *Asperula   odorata,*   Bed - straw

29. Woodruff.   30. Thyme-leaved Speedwell.

family.   The erect stem is $\frac{1}{2}$ to 1 ft. high, with whorls of about 6 to 8 stiff lance-shaped leaves : the small white flowers are gathered in loose terminal groups : the plant is very fragrant, especially when dry : common in woods, flowering in early summer.

30. **Thyme - leaved Speedwell,** *Veronica serpyllifolia,* Fox-glove family.   This little plant is a common weed in gardens, woods, and roadsides : the branched stem lies along the ground, and has pairs of smooth, oval leaves ; the terminal portion of each branch is, however, erect, and bears a single spike of flowers ; the flowers, which are small and white, with delicate blue veins, appear throughout summer.

31. **Eye-bright,** *Euphrasia officinalis,* Foxglove

family. A very variable little plant, common on heaths and pastures, where it flowers in summer : it may range from 1 to 8 ins. in height, the stem being simple or slightly branched, and bearing pairs of ovate, serrate, sessile leaves : the flowers form a short, terminal spike : in colour they may be white, white veined with purple, or completely purple.

32. **Wood-sage,** *Teucrium Scorodonia,* Dead-

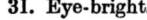

31. Eye-bright.   32. Wood-sage.

nettle family. The stem is square and about 1 ft. high, with pairs of wrinkled, ovate or heart-shaped leaves, the margins of which are bluntly serrate : the flowers are rather small, tubular, dirty-white in colour, and occur in two or three terminal spikes : the plant, which has an aromatic smell if crushed, flowers in late summer, and is common in dry woods and on banks.

33. **Spring Whitlow-grass,** *Erophila verna,* Cress family. This pretty little plant occurs in patches

on walls and bare, dry banks, and in spring speckles
them with the white of its starry flowers : the flower-
stalks rise from a rosette of
lance-shaped, toothed leaves,
and are either simple, with one
or two flowers, or may carry
several little spikes : each petal
is deeply divided into two lobes :
the plant is usually less than 2
ins. high, but may sometimes
reach a height of about 4 ins.

33. Spring Whitlow-
grass.

34. **Scurvy-grass,** *Cochlearia
officinalis,* Cress family. A
plant of the sea-coast, flowering on grassy slopes,
and in crevices of the cliffs, in spring and summer : the leaves are smooth and rather fleshy,

34. Scurvy-grass.

35. Jack-by-the-Hedge.

those at the base of the stem being more or less
heart-shaped, while the leaves of the flowering stems
have no stalks, and tend to be arrow-shaped :

the flowers occur in dense spikes : the plant was
formerly used as a cure for and preventive of scurvy
by whalers and Arctic travellers.

35. Jack-by-the-Hedge, Sauce-alone, *Sisymbrium Alliaria*, Cress family. A tall plant (1 to 3 ft.)
of hedges and damp woods : the stem is slender,
with large, thin, light-green leaves, the upper heart-
shaped and coarsely toothed, the lower more rounded :

36. Pepperwort.   37. Penny-Cress.

the small flowers are gathered in short spikes, and
appear in early summer : the plant smells of garlic
when crushed.

36. **Pepperwort**, *Lepidium Smithii*, Cress family.
A common weed of dry banks, flowering in summer :
the stem is ½ to 1 ft. high, and is closely clad with
arrow-shaped, sessile leaves : the lower leaves are
narrowed into a stalk : the flowers are small and
gathered in short thick spikes : the fruit is an ovate
pouch with an apical notch : the plant is rough with
hairs.

37. Penny-Cress, *Thlaspi arvense,* Cress family.
The stem, which is about 1 ft. high, is loosely clad
with arrow-shaped leaves: the small white flowers
are gathered in loose spikes: the most notable
feature is the fruit, which gives the plant its name;
it is a large disc-shaped pouch, with the centre
swollen, and with an apical notch: a common field
weed, flowering in summer.

38. Grass of Parnassus.   39. Sundew.

38. Grass of Parnassus, *Parnassia palustris,*
Saxifrage family. A very beautiful and not uncommon bog plant, flowering in autumn: it has a
rosette of stalked heart-shaped leaves, from which
rise the flowering stems: the leaves on the stems
are sessile: the flowers are large and creamy white:
the plant is about ¾ ft. high, and is quite smooth.

39. Sundew, *Drosera rotundifolia,* Sundew family.
A little bog plant, readily recognised by its rosette
of round, stalked leaves, which are covered with
small, red tentacles, and have a glistening appear-

ance, as if spangled with dew: any insect which
lights on the leaf is held by a sticky fluid, and the
tentacles close over it, pouring on to it a digestive

40. Chickweed Wintergreen.   41. Comfrey.

liquid, which enables the plant to absorb the nutri-
tious part of its prey: the *Sundew* is thus *insectiv-
orous*: the small, whitish flowers are borne in little
clusters on stalks, rising from the rosette in late
summer.

40. Chickweed Wintergreen, *Trientalis europœa,*
Primrose family.   The stem is about 4 ins. high, and
bears a single whorl of pointed leaves, oval in shape,
but broadest towards the tip: from this spring several
delicate flower-stalks, each with a fairly large, white,
star-like flower: the plant is a very beautiful, but
by no means common inhabitant of northern woods,
flowering in early summer.

41. Comfrey, *Symphytum officinale,* Forget-me-not
family.   A tall (1 to 2 ft.) coarse plant, common in

damp, shady places : the large lance-shaped leaves
are continued down the stem in the form of prominent
ridges : the flowers occur in small, drooping clusters
in the leaf-axils : they are bell-shaped, usually
white, but sometimes purple, and appear in early
summer : the whole plant is very rough with hairs.

42. **Ramsons, Wild Garlic,** *Allium ursinum*,
Hyacinth family. From the subterranean bulb
arise two large, soft, oval, pointed leaves, and a long
triangular flower-stalk, which bears a single umbel
of large white flowers ; below these are two mem-
branous leaves : the whole plant gives off a smell of
garlic if crushed : it is fairly common in damp woods,
often occurring in large patches : flowers in early
summer.

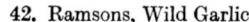

42. Ramsons, Wild Garlic.   43. Mouse-ear.

43. **Mouse-ear,** *Cerastium vulgatum*, Pink family.
An insignificant little weed of the garden, the field,
and the roadside : the branches of the stem are

mostly prostrate, but some rise from the ground,
and these bear groups of small white flowers, the

44. Water-Lily.　　　　45. Chickweed.

petals of which are almost hidden within the calyx:
the leaves are in pairs, lance-shaped, and, like the

46. Greater Stitchwort.　　　47. Pearlwort.

whole plant, more or less downy: flowers almost
the whole year through.

44. Water-Lily, *Castalia alba,* Water-lily family. The most striking of our water plants : the large white flowers appear on the surface of the water in August : it is of interest to note that the petals pass gradually into the stamens : the seeds are liberated only when the fruit rots away : the leaves are large, floating, and rounded heart-shaped.

48. Spurrey.   49. Wintergreen.

45. Chickweed, *Stellaria media,* Pink family. A common garden weed : the stem is much branched, and often reaches a considerable length, trailing on the ground : the leaves are in pairs, ovate and bright green : the flowers occur singly in the leaf axils, as well as in little groups at the tips of the stems ; they are small, and the petals, which are hidden in the calyx, are cleft in two almost to the base : flowers throughout the year.

46. Greater Stitchwort, *Stellaria Holostea,* Pink family. A handsome, early summer plant : the weak stems, about 1 to 2 ft. long, generally grow in the rough grass of hedges and banks, which supports them : the leaves are in pairs, lance-shaped, drawn out, and rough : flowers large, white, in terminal groups. The *Lesser Stitchwort* is a more slender plant flowering in summer. The *Marsh Stitchwort* is found in wet places, and has quite small flowers.

47. Pearlwort, *Sagina nodosa,* Pink family.   The

stems occur in a group, are at first prostrate, and then rise to a height of 3 to 4 ins., bearing each 1 to 3 flowers : the flowers are large, delicate, and white : the leaves are short and narrow, and occur 2 to 4 together on the stems : a fresh little plant, common in moist places, flowering in summer : it has one or two similar relatives, with inconspicuous flowers having only 4 stamens.

48. Spurrey, *Spergula arvensis,* Pink family.   The

50. Arrowhead.

stem is about 1 ft. high, with whorls of long narrow leaves, each with a furrow along its lower face : the flowers are of medium size, and are gathered in loose, leafless spikes at the end of the stems ; when the fruit is formed the flower-stalks bend downwards : a common weed of cultivated land, flowering in summer, and emitting an evil stench, especially when wet with dew or rain : it occurs in two varieties, the commoner of which has frequently fewer stamens —often only 5.

49. Wintergreen, *Pyrola minor,* Heath family.

The stem is prostrate for a short distance, and bears
several rounded oval leaves, then it bends sharply
upwards, and ends in a slender spike of drooping
flowers, almost globular in shape, and in colour
white, with a shade of pink : a pretty summer flower,
found in woods and heaths.

50. Arrowhead, *Sagittaria sagittifolia,* Water-
plantain family.   A plant of English ditches and
rivers : the leaves rise from the water on long stalks,
and are arrow-shaped : in the centre of these is
the tall flower-stalk, with a spike of large, white
flowers, some of which have only stamens, and others
only seed-vessels : many leaves remain submerged,
and these possess only long narrow stalks without
blades : flowers in August.

YELLOW FLOWERS,
51–99.

I. Flowers grouped in Composite Heads . . . 51–65
II. Flowers grouped otherwise or occurring singly . 66–99

    A. Leaves compound, deeply cut, or lobed . 66–80
    B. Leaves quite simple, at most toothed . 81–99

        a. Stamens absent, or 3 or 4 in number 81–86
        b. Stamens 5 or 6 in number . . . 87–90
        c. Stamens more than 6 in number . 91–99

51. Golden-rod, *Solidago Virgaurea,* Daisy family.

The leaves are lance-shaped
with serrate edges, dark green
in colour, and borne on the an-
gular branched stem: flower-
heads small but numerous,
and gathered into a handsome,
yellow, brush-like inflorescence : the plant is medium-
sized, 1 to 2 ft. high, and in-
clined to be bushy : it grows
in thickets, flowering in late
summer : the leaves were formerly much used for dressing
wounds: foreign species are
cultivated as the *Golden-rods*
of the garden.

51. Golden-rod.

52. Corn-Marigold, *Chrysan-*
themum segetum, Daisy family. The leaves are very

40

smooth, and bright green, oblong in shape, but deeply notched : flower-heads large, with a conspicuous ray, and occurring singly : the plant is small, about 1 ft. high, and slightly branched : it occurs in corn-fields, where it flowers from June to August : not originally a native in Britain, but now completely at home.

53. **Tansy**, *Tanacetum vulgare*, Daisy family.   The

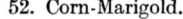

52. Corn-Marigold.   53. Tansy.

leaf is deeply feather-cut into slender segments ; these are again divided, and the segments so formed are serrate ; in consequence the whole leaf has a feathery appearance. The flower-heads are small, button-like, and have no ray : they occur in large, flat, umbel-like inflorescences : the plant is 2 to 3 ft. high, and has a handsome appearance : it grows about roadsides and river-banks, and is cultivated in old gardens for the sake of its strong aroma. *Tansy*

Tea, made from the leaves, was formerly a much used " simple."

‣ **54. Coltsfoot,** *Tussilago Farfara,* Daisy family. This plant possesses an underground stem, which lives through the winter, and in March sends up a short stalk, clothed with small, pointed, reddish scales, with a single large, bright yellow flower-head : in early spring these are conspicuous and beautiful along roads, railways, and field-sides : the leaves

54. Coltsfoot.   55. Groundsel.

only appear when the flower is over : they are large, roundish heart-shaped, with toothed margins : the under surface is covered with a white down : the leaf is still used as a substitute for tobacco, and is supposed to be a cure for colds.

55. Groundsel, *Senecio vulgaris,* Daisy family. The leaves are smooth and sometimes woolly, cut into blunt, toothed lobes : the flower-heads are small, somewhat egg-shaped, without a ray, and occur a few together at the apex of the stem : the plant is a weed of cultivated land, and particularly of gardens : its only use is as a food for canaries : *Senecio sylvaticus* is a very similar plant, growing by roadsides : it may be distinguished by its sticky stem, woolly leaves, and by its disagreeable smell.

56. Ragwort, *Senecio Jacobæa,* Daisy family. A tall, coarse plant which grows on commons and pastures : it is sometimes called the *Tansy,* but is readily

56. Ragwort.   57. Nipplewort.

distinguished from that plant : it has no aroma : its flower-heads have a distinct ray, and are gathered into a large and conspicuous head : the leaves are deeply cut into toothed lobes, but have not the feathery appearance of those of *Tanacetum :* a handsome plant, but an annoying weed : *S. aquaticus* is a similar plant which grows in boggy situations.

57. Nipplewort, *Lapsana communis,* Daisy family. The lower leaves are lyre-shaped, with one large, ovate terminal lobe and several pairs of smaller lobes : the stem is slender, about 2 ft. high, branched, and stem and leaves are slightly hairy : the flower-heads are small and gathered into a loose terminal

58. Hawk's-beard.   59. Mouse-ear Hawkweed.

inflorescence : the fruit has no pappus (see *Hypo-chœris*) : the plant is common in shady places, where it flowers in late summer.

58. Hawk's-beard, *Crepis virens,* Daisy family. A slender branched plant of medium size, common in meadows, where it flowers in summer : the upper leaves are arrow-shaped, and clasp the stem ; the lower are frequently cut into blunt segments, or they may only have large, narrow teeth : the leaves are all smooth : the flower-heads are smallish, and occur in a loose brush : *C. paludosa* is a larger-flowered species, with dandelion-like leaves, which grows in marshy ground.

59. Mouse-ear Hawkweed, *Hieracium Pilosella,* Daisy family. The leaves form a rosette on ·the surface of the ground ; they are oval and pointed, very hairy on both sides, and white underneath : the flower-heads are fairly large, and occur singly on the end of stalks 3 to 4 ins. high, several of which may rise from the centre of the rosette ; the rosette also gives rise to leafy runners : the plant is common on dry sunny banks, and flowers all summer.

60. **Hawkweed,** *Hieracium boreale,* Daisy family. A tall (2 to 4 ft.), handsome plant, with large yellow flower-heads, gathered into a loose apical inflorescence : the stem is leafy and branched, the leaves toothed, ovate or lance-shaped, the upper sessile, the lower narrowed into a stalk : flowers about August, and is common in dry sunny situations. There is a very large number of different species of

60. Hawkweed.   61. Cat's-ear.

Hawkweed, many of which differ only slightly from each other.

61. **Cat's-ear,** *Hypochœris radicata,* Daisy family. The leaves form a rosette : they are oblong, with

large, blunt teeth pointing backwards, and covered with short rough hairs ; the stem is about 1 ft. high, is branched, and has only very small leaves : the flower-heads are large, and occur singly at the apices of the stem branches : like most other members of the daisy family, the little, seed-like fruits are crowned by a circle of fine hairs—the "*pappus* "—which represents the calyx of the flower : this pappus enables the fruit to remain long suspended in the air, so that it may be borne a considerable distance by the wind, and settle in a new position far from the parent plant : in the case of the *Cat's-ear* (and some others), the pappus is borne, not on the fruit itself, but on a slender beak situated on the apex of the fruit : it has the appearance of a tiny umbrella : the *Cat's-ear* grows on waste ground, and flowers in July.

62. Hawkbit.

62. Hawkbit, *Leontodon autumnalis*, Daisy family. Closely resembles the *Cat's-ear*, but may be distinguished from it by the pappus, which rests on the fruit, and by the fact that the leaves are narrower, more deeply cut, and not so hairy : found in pastures and waste ground, flowering all summer.

63. Dandelion, *Taraxacum officinale*, Daisy family. The leaves of this familiar meadow and roadside plant are long, pointed, bright glossy green, and have large teeth pointing backwards : they are arranged in a rosette from which spring the hollow flower-stalks, each with its single, large, bright yellow head: as conspicuous as the flower-head is the fruiting-head, which succeeds it: each little seed-like fruit is provided with an umbrella-like pappus, and the whole head—the material of a familiar game in every country—is a dainty ball of plumes.

64. Sowthistle, *Sonchus oleraceus*, Daisy family. A tall, coarse plant, with a thick, somewhat branched

63. Dandelion.

64. Sowthistle.

stem: little bunches of the large, bright yellow flower-heads are borne about the tips of the branches: the leaves and stem have a strikingly glossy, dark-green appearance: the upper leaves are arrow-shaped, sharply toothed, and clasp the stem: the lower leaves may be lobed: flowers in summer, being abundant on waste ground.

65. Goat's-beard, Jack-go-to-bed-at-noon, *Tragopogon pratense*, Daisy family. The leaves are long, narrow, and sharply pointed: the stem is about 18 ins. high, and is branched: at the tips of the branches are borne the large, yellow flower-heads, which only open in the early morning, closing about eleven o'clock : the pappus (see *Hypochœris*) is very conspicuous, and is borne on the end of a long beak : common in pastures, flowering in June.

65. Goat's-beard, Jack-go-to-bed-at-noon.

66. Upright Crowfoot, Buttercup, *Ranunculus acris*, Crowfoot family. The bright yellow flowers of the *Buttercup* are familiar in all meadows : they appear in summer on stems 1 to 2 ft. high : most of the leaves grow on long stalks from near the root : they are hairy and deeply palm-divided, the segments being also cut : the flower-stalks are not furrowed. There are several related species which are quite common : the *Creeping Crowfoot*, with a furrowed flower-stalk, and sending out runners : the *Bulbous Crowfoot*, with the sepals bent sharply back, and the base of the stem much swollen : *Goldilocks*, common in woods, distinguished from the others by the fact that there is no little scale inside the petals at their base : the *Corn Crowfoot*, in cornfields, with spiny seed-vessels.

66. Upright Crowfoot, Buttercup.

67. Greater Celandine, *Chelidonium majus*,

Poppy family. The stem is tall, branched, and leafy : the leaves are fairly large and deeply lobed : the flowers are small, and the fruits long and pod-like : the plant is common in shady waste places, and is peculiar in possessing a thick juice, which is bright orange in colour : flowers in summer.

68. Yellow Rocket, *Barbarea vulgaris*, Cress family. The stem is 1 to 2 ft. high, and may be slightly branched : the leaves are feather-lobed, lyre-shaped, and dark, glossy green : the flowers are small, yellow, and borne in crowded spikes at the ends of the branches : the fruits are long slender pods containing many seeds : a common weed of waste places and cultivated fields, flowering throughout summer.

67. Greater Celandine.

69. Charlock, *Brassica arvensis*, Cress family. This " wild mustard " is an exceedingly common weed in corn-fields : it flowers in summer, when the corn is still green, and sometimes turns whole fields into a mass of gold : the stem is about 1½ ft. high : the upper leaves are ovate, notched, and sessile ; the lower have stalks and are feather-lobed : the flowers occur in terminal spikes : the pods are knotty.

68. Yellow Rocket.

70. Mignonette, *Reseda lutea*, Mignonette family.
The wild *Mignonette* is not unlike the garden sort,

69. Charlock.   70. Mignonette.

but it is odourless: the stem is taller, and the
flowers are yellow with a greenish tinge: they are
 borne in spikes at the end
of the leafy stem: the leaves
are much cut, and are smooth:
the seed-vessel is peculiar, as
it is always open: the *Weld*
is a close relative; it is a
taller, coarser plant with green
flowers; both plants are common on waste ground, flowering in summer.

71. Black Medick.

    71. Black Medick, *Medicago
lupulina*, Pea family.   Many
tiny yellow flowers are gath-
ered in little oval heads, borne on short stalks

along the stem: the leaves have 3 leaflets, which are toothed: stipules small, toothed: the fruit is a little, curved pod, green at first, then black: the teeth of the calyx are' equal in length: the plant is quite small, and trails along the ground: common on waste ground, flowering throughout the summer.

72. Melilot.

72. Melilot, *Melilotus officinalis*, Pea family. The stems are erect, 2 to 3 ft. high: the leaves have 3 elliptical, serrate leaflets, and small, sharply-pointed stipules: the flowers are small, and borne in long slender spikes, in the leaf axils, on the upper part of the stems: the plant is common in dry pastures, flowering in summer: it has a delightful, sweet, aromatic odour, especially when dry, and is used in flavouring gruyère cheese.

73. Hop Trefoil.

73. Hop Trefoil, *Trifolium procumbens*, Pea family. The flowers are crowded into little stalked heads of about 40: the leaves have 3 leaflets: the stem is trailing: 2 of the calyx teeth are much shorter than the other 3: the stipules are entire: common about roadsides and other dry places, flowering in summer: the *Lesser Trefoil* is a smaller species with only about a dozen flowers in the heads, and resembles the Medick, from which it may be distinguished by the character of the pod, which remains hidden within the withered corolla.

74. Lady's Finger, Kidney Vetch, *Anthyllis Vulneraria,* Pea family. Several short (6 to 12 ins.) stems rise close together from the root : the feather-compound leaves have 7 to 11 leaflets, and are soft with hairs : the pale-yellow flowers are gathered in

74. Lady's Finger, Kidney   75. Bird's-foot Trefoil.
         Vetch.

heads, 2 heads always standing together at the tip of a branch : common on dry banks, flowering in summer : the leaves were formerly used for dressing wounds.

75. Bird's-foot Trefoil, *Lotus corniculatus,* Pea family. Another creeping plant, with orange-yellow flowers gathered in heads : the flowers are, however, large, and only 5 to 10 occur in a head : the stalk which bears the head is long and slender : the pod is long and narrow : the leaves have 3 leaflets, but appear to have 5, because the stipules are large and resemble leaflets : the leaflets are sharply pointed : the plant is common in dry pastures, flowers in summer, and has a pleasant odour.

76. **Meadow Vetchling,** *Lathyrus pratensis*, Pea family. The stem may be a yard long, and rambles over the banks on which the plant grows : the leaves have 2 lance-shaped leaflets, and 2 fairly large

76. Meadow Vetchling.   77. Wood Avens.

stipules : the tip of the leaf is converted into a delicate branched tendril, which aids the plant in climbing : the flowers occur several together in loose heads, borne on long stalks, in the leaf axils : flowers in late summer.

77. **Wood Avens,** *Geum urbanum*, Rose family. The stem is about 2 ft. high, and is branched : the small yellow flowers occur singly about the tips of the branches : the leaves are lyre-shaped ; leaflets serrate ; stipules prominent. The little seed-like

fruit, when ripe, is provided with a hooked spine, by which it becomes attached to passing animals, and is carried off to a new situation : it is common in woods and thickets, flowering in summer.

78. Tormentil.   79. Silver-weed.

78. Tormentil, *Potentilla sylvestris,* Rose family. The stem is trailing, and arises from a woody stock : the leaves are palm-compound, the upper sessile, the lower stalked ; leaflets serrate ; stipules prominent : the flowers are small, with slender stalks, and stand singly in the leaf axils : common on dry banks, flowering in summer : the woody stock has been used in medicine, and for dyeing.

79. Silver-weed, *Potentilla Anserina,* Rose family. The stem is creeping, and bears feather-compound leaves, with many serrate leaflets ; these are not all of one size, smaller alternate with larger : the leaves are of a silvery white colour beneath : the flowers are large, and occur singly : the plant is a common weed of roadsides, flowering in early summer : the root is eaten by pigs.

80. Agrimony, *Agrimonia Eupatoria,* Rose family.
The stem is erect and of medium height : the feather-
compound leaves have about 7 large leaflets, and
a number of intermediate small ones : leaflets are
sharply serrate and hairy : the flowers are small,
and pale yellow, and are borne on a long slender
terminal spike : the plant grows on dry sunny banks
and fields, and flowers in summer : formerly used
for medicinal purposes. *A. odorata,* a similar plant
with a fragrant odour, is much rarer.

81. Crosswort, *Galium cruciata,* Bed-straw family.
The stem is 1 to 2 ft. long, and is somewhat weak, so
that the plant tends to trail in the coarse grass or
bushes amongst which it grows : the leaves are
numerous, and are arranged in whorls of 4 ; they are
oval and hairy : in the axils of the upper whorls are
groups of flowers : the flower is small, pale yellow,

80. Agrimony.   81. Crosswort.

and shaped like a four-rayed star : flowers in spring
and early summer.

82. Yellow Bed-straw, *Galium verum,* Bed-straw

family. The stem is erect, about 1 to 1½ ft. high :
the leaves are numerous, and occur in whorls
of about 8 : they are very narrow, needle-shaped,
and dark, glossy green : the flowers are like those of
the *Crosswort*, but are bright yellow, and occur in
a conspicuous, crowded brush at the end of the stem,
giving the plant a striking appearance on the dry
banks and turfy places, where it flowers in summer.

83. **Yellow Toad-flax,** *Linaria vulgaris*, Fox-glove

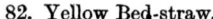

82. Yellow Bed-straw.   83. Yellow Toad-flax.

family. The stem is 1 to 2 ft. high, clad with
dark, smooth, narrow leaves, and ending in a handsome spike of flowers : the flowers are large and yellow,
with an orange spot : the corolla is in one piece,
with 2 lips, the lower lip being pursed up so as to
close the opening : it is provided with a honey-
containing spur behind : found on gravelly soil,
flowering in summer.

84. **Musk,** *Mimulus Langsdorfii*, Foxglove family.
This plant is found commonly on the margins of
ponds and ditches : it has a thick stem 1 to 2 ft.

high, which bears large, smooth, ovate leaves with serrate edges : the flowers are large, bright yellow, and occur at the tip of the stem : the plant is a native of America, but is now quite acclimatised and widely spread in this country ; it flowers throughout summer.

85. Yellow Rattle, *Rhinanthus Crista-galli,* Foxglove family.   The stem is 1 to 2 ft. high, and bears many pairs of lance-shaped, sharply serrate leaves :

84. Musk.   85. Yellow Rattle.

the flowers are in a loose terminal spike : the yellow corolla protrudes only slightly from the bladder-like calyx : the plant is common in pastures, flowering in summer, and is interesting because it attaches its roots to those of grasses, and draws nourishment from these.

86. Spotted Hemp-nettle, *Galeopsis versicolor,* Dead-nettle family.   This is one of the most striking weeds of cultivated ground, being specially abundant in potato and turnip fields : it is at once distinguished by its tall (2 to 3 ft. high), square, branched stem, and its large, yellow, purple-spotted flowers, with their 2-lipped corollas : the leaves are ovate, with a narrow point and serrate margin, and are borne in pairs : flowers in autumn.

87. Primrose, *Primula vulgaris*, Primrose family. The primrose is one of our most typical spring flowers : it is to be found in all sorts of positions, from dry sunny banks to damp woods, flowering as

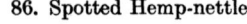

86. Spotted Hemp-nettle.   87. Primrose.

early as March : the oblong, wrinkled leaves form a rosette on the ground, from which rise the flower-stalks, each with a single flower : the flowers are of two kinds : in one, called *thrum-eyed*, the little bunch of 5 stamens appears in the opening of the salver-shaped corolla : in the other, the *pin-eyed*, found on a different plant, the opening is closed by the pinhead-like stigma : this is an adaptation to secure cross-fertilisation, as the part of an insect which touches the stamens of the one kind of flower will touch the stigma of the other kind only : *Primula veris*, the *Cowslip*, has a little bunch of smaller and darker yellow stalked flowers at the tip of a common stem.

88. **Loosestrife,** *Lysimachia vulgaris*, Primrose family. A tall plant, 2 to 3 ft. high, flowering on stream banks in July : the leaves are large, ovate, and borne in groups of 2, 3, or 4 : the yellow flowers occur in a dense terminal pyramid.

89. Yellow Pimpernel, *Lysimachia nemorum*, Primrose family. A little creeping plant found in damp woods : the stem bears pairs of glossy, ovate leaves, from the

88. Loosestrife.

axils of which spring slender stalks, each with a single small, starry, yellow flower, later on replaced

by a globular seed-vessel. *L. Nummularia*, the *Moneywort*, grows in similar situations : its leaves are broader, and its flowers, on shorter stalks, are much larger; altogether a more striking species : both flower in summer.

90. Bog-Asphodel, *Narthecium ossifragum*, Hyacinth family. A pretty little plant about 6 ins. high, common in peat-bogs, flowering in summer : the single stem bears a spike of golden yellow flowers and a few short leaves : from the lower part

89. Yellow Pimpernel.

of the stem spring groups of grass-like sword-shaped leaves.

91. Lesser Spearwort, *Ranunculus Flammula,* Crowfoot family. Growing in wet places along the margins of streams and lakes, the *Spearwort* has an upright stem, about 1 to 1½ ft. high, bearing leaves, the lower ovate, the upper quite narrow ; they are entire and smooth : the flowers are few in number, bright yellow, and about ½ in. across : the juice of

90. Bog-Asphodel.   91. Lesser Spearwort.

the plant acts as a strong irritant on the skin : flowers in summer : the *Greater Spearwort* is a rarer plant, with much larger flowers.

92. Lesser Celandine, *Ranunculus Ficaria,* Crowfoot family. This beautiful spring flower carpets the forest floor with golden flowers in March and April, and with glossy green leaves in early summer : the leaves are roundish, heart-shaped, stalked, and in a rosette, from which rise the flower-stalks, each with a single bright yellow flower : the roots, which

persist during winter, are tuberous, and carry a store
of food, thus enabling the plant to produce flowers
and leaves early in the year.

92. Lesser Celandine.

93. Marsh-Marigold.

93. Marsh-Marigold, *Caltha palustris,* Crowfoot
family. The large yellow flowers of this handsome
plant appear in spring, borne
at the tip of the hollow
stem: the plant is frequent
in marshes and ditches: the
leaves are rounded, heart-
shaped, and dark glossy green;
there is no corolla, the calyx
taking its place.

**94. Yellow Water - Lily,
Brandy - Bottle,** *Nymphœa
lutea,* Water-lily family. The
leaves are elongated, heart-
shaped; they are unwet-
table, and float on the surface of the water, while the
plant roots in the mud below:

94. Yellow Water-Lily,
Brandy-Bottle.

the flowers appear in July, and are large, with a
smell like brandy: the seed-vessel is urn-shaped.

95. Rock-Rose ; *Helianthemum Chamæcistus,* Rock-rose family. This is a common plant on dry

banks and pastures : it is small, low-growing, and some-what shrubby : the stems bear pairs of small, oval, slightly hairy leaves, with stipules, and a few large, bright yellow flowers, with fragile petals : flowers in summer and autumn.

96. St. John's Wort, *Hy-pericum pulchrum,* St. John's

95. Rock-Rose.

Wort family. The loose spikes of the small yellow flowers, with reddish buds and stamens, are a common feature of our heaths and

hedges in summer : the slender stem may be slightly branched, and has pairs of small, sessile, heart-shaped leaves : the small black dots on the petals and sepals are glands : several other species, all with spikes of yellow flowers, but differing in vari-ous respects, are common.

97. Petty Whin, *Genista anglica,* Vetch family. On heather moors, in moist but not boggy positions, the *Petty Whin* is frequently found : it is a little plant with a trailing, slightly branched stem : the leaves are small

96. St. John's Wort.

and ovate, and, besides these, the stem bears slender compound thorns, which are modified branches : the flowers are fairly large, occurring in loose clusters in early summer: the pods are much swollen when ripe. *G. tinctoria,* a less common species, without thorns and with elliptic leaves, goes by the name of *Dyer's-weed,* as it yields a yellow dye.

98. Furze, Gorse, Whin, *Ulex europœus,* Vetch family. The *Whin* is very common on heaths, pastures, and waste places, and lends a note of

97. Petty Whin.   98. Furze, Gorse, Whin.

colour to the countryside in the early months of the year, when it begins to flower : the leaves and many of the branches are reduced to the characteristic spines—this at the same time preventing loss of much water, and protecting the shrub from browsing animals : the large yellow flowers and their peculiar fragrance are familiar to all.

99. Wall-Pepper, Biting Stonecrop, *Sedum acre,* Stone-crop family. This little plant is common in dry rocky places : in such situations it is exposed to

great drought, but its little, cylindrical, fleshy leaves
act as water-stores, and only dry up with great
difficulty : if chewed they have a flavour of pepper :
the flowers are star-like and yellow, appearing in
summer.

99. Wall-Pepper, Biting
Stonecrop.

ROSE FLOWERS,
100–116.

A. Leaves compound, deeply cut, or lobed . **100–104**
B. Leaves quite simple, at most toothed . 105–116

100. Fumitory, *Fumaria officinalis,* Fumitory family. A common weed of cultivated land : the

100. Fumitory.   101. Rest-harrow.

stem is low, weak, and much branched, so that the plant has a bushy appearance : the leaves are bright green, and twice compound : the flowers, which are small and gathered in little spikes at the ends of the

branches, have a little spur, so that they appear to
be fixed sideways on the stalk : the tips of the petals

102. Water Avens.   103. Buckbean.

are often darker than the rest of the flower : flowers
throughout the summer ; a graceful plant.

104. Red Rattle.   105. Maiden Pink.

101. Rest-harrow, *Ononis repens,* Vetch family.
The prostrate, branched, and often somewhat woody

stem grows along the sand and turf of dunes and similar barren situations : the leaves are compound, with 3 leaflets, and usually the plant is provided with a few spines : the flowers, which occur singly in the leaf-axils, are fairly large, and rose-pink, veined with crimson ; they appear throughout summer.

102. Water Avens, *Geum rivale,* Rose family. Stem is 1 to 1½ ft. high : the leaves are feather-

| 106. Ragged Robin. | 107. Cat's-Foot, Mountain Everlasting. |

compound, with 1 large terminal leaflet and several pairs of smaller ones : at the apex of the stem are borne a few flowers : these are large, drooping, and in colour rose, tinged with brown ; they open in summer : the whole plant is hairy, the fruits are distributed by small animals, to which they become attached by a hooked bristle : a plant of damp meadows.

103. Buckbean, *Menyanthes trifoliata,* Gentian family. A very beautiful plant of boggy ground :

the thick round stem generally lies under water, and
gives off the leaves, which have long stalks, and 3
serrate oval leaflets, and the flower-stalk, at the
apex of which is a spike of large, pale rose flowers :

the inner side of the petals
is covered with delicate white
hairs : flowers in early
summer.

104. Red Rattle, *Pedicularis
sylvatica,* Foxglove family. A
little plant (4 to 6 ins.) of
moist woods and heaths : the
stem branches at the base,
and the prostrate branches
rise at the tips, holding up
short spikes of large rose-
coloured flowers : the leaves
are deeply cut into many
notched segments : flowers in
summer : the *Lousewort* (*P.*

108. Cross-leaved Heath.   *palustris*) is a similar but
larger and more erect plant,
with brighter flowers, common in bogs.

105. Maiden Pink, *Dianthus deltoides,* Pink family.
A very beautiful but rather rare little plant, of dry
turfy ground : the stem is much branched below,
and bears many pairs of small, narrow leaves : the
flowers are fairly large, of exactly the form of our
single garden pinks, bright rose-coloured, with a
darker " eye," and scentless : flowers in summer
and autumn.

106. Ragged Robin, *Lychnis Flos-cuculi,* Pink
family. The tall slender stems and spikes of large
pink flowers of this plant are common and beautiful
objects on marshy ground : the leaves occur in
pairs, and are lance-shaped, the lower ones narrowed

towards the base : the edges of the petals are cut
into a fringe, giving the flower its " ragged " appearance : the stem is sticky : flowers in early summer.

107. Cat's-foot, Mountain Everlasting, *Antennaria
dioica*, Daisy family. The little creeping stem bears
many small oval leaves, broadest towards the tip,
shiny above, and silvery, with hairs on the lower
surface : from it arises a simple flowering stem,

109. Thrift, Sea-Daisy.   110. Centaury.

about 4 to 6 ins. high, with 4 or 5 small flower-heads,
pale rose or white in colour : common on heaths,
flowering in summer.

108. Cross-leaved Heath, *Erica Tetralix*, Heath
family. A common plant of boggy heaths, flowering
in late summer and autumn : it is most readily
distinguished from the other common heaths by its
drooping cluster of large, egg-shaped, pale rose
flowers : the stem is 6 to 8 ins. high, and bears
many whorls of 4 small, narrow, hairy leaves, and
at its apex the drooping cluster of flowers.

109. Thrift, Sea-Daisy, *Statice maritima,* Thrift family. A common plant of grassy slopes and clefts of rocks near the sea : the woody stock gives rise to

111. Bindweed.   112. Knot-Grass.

a tuft of grass-like but rather fleshy leaves, and to one or more flower-stalks : the flower-stalk is 6 to 8 ins. high, and bears a single globular head of rose flowers : flowers from spring to autumn.

110. Centaury, *Erythræa Centaurium,* Gentian family. The stem is about a foot high, and is square, bearing pairs of smooth elliptical leaves : towards the apex it is slightly branched, and has a large, flat brush of bright rose-coloured flowers, individually small, but making a handsome show in the mass : flowers in late summer, and not uncommon on dry waste ground and pastures. *E. littoralis* is a similar, but smaller and rarer plant, growing by the sea.

111. Bindweed, *Convolvulus arvensis,* Bindweed family. The stem is slender, and twines through

grass and hedges : the leaves are halbert-shaped and
stalked : the flowers are large, shaped like an open
bell, in colour white, variegated with pink : flowers
in summer. *C. sepium*, the *Great Bindweed*, has
very large white flowers and arrow-shaped leaves.
C. Soldanella, the *Sea Bindweed*, is less common : it
has fleshy, kidney-shaped leaves and handsome pink
and yellow flowers.

112. **Knot-Grass,** *Polygonum aviculare*, Dock
family. A very common weed of cultivated and
waste ground : the long, branched, creeping stems
bear many small elliptical leaves, each with a mem-
branous sheath at the base : in the axils of the
leaves are little groups of small pink flowers, tinged
with green : flowers from spring to autumn.

113. **Spotted Persicaria,** *Polygonum Persicaria,*

113. Spotted Persicaria.   114. Amphibious Persicaria.

Dock family. A common weed of cultivated land :
the stem is about 1 ft. high and generally somewhat
prostrate : the leaves are fairly large, lance-shaped,

provided with a fringed sheath, smooth, dark green,
and often spotted with dark brownish purple: the
flowers are arranged in close spikes, in the leaf axils
and at the apex of the stem; they are pale rose-
coloured, appearing in summer and autumn.

114. **Amphibious Persicaria,** *Polygonum amphib-
ium,* Dock family. This plant is an inhabitant of
ponds and ditches, and according as it grows actually

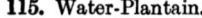

115. Water-Plantain.   116. Flowering-Rush.

in the water or only along the water's edge, it produces different types of leaves: in the water the
leaves are oblong, dark glossy green, and unwettable,
so that they float on the surface: on land they are
lance-shaped, lighter green, and slightly hairy: the
flowers are pale rose, and gathered in close terminal
spikes; they appear in late summer and autumn.

115. **Water-Plantain,** *Alisma Plantago-aquatica,*
Water-Plantain family. A plant of the boggy margins of ponds and lakes, flowering in late summer:

the tall, slender stem bears a large, loose brush of small, pale rose flowers : the leaves are large, ovate or lance-shaped, with long stalks, but any growing under water are quite narrow.

116. Flowering-Rush, *Butomus umbellatus,* Water-Plantain family. A very beautiful inhabitant of the margins of ponds and slow streams : the stem is short, horizontal, and roots in the mud : it sends up a number of long, narrow leaves, and in summer a tall flowering stem (2 to 3 ft.), with a single, terminal umbel of large rose-flowers.

RED FLOWERS,

117–121.

117. Poppy, Corn-Rose, *Papaver Rhœas,* Poppy family. Stem 1 to 2 ft. high, rough with hairs : the leaves are oval and deeply feather-divided into notched segments : the flowers are large, with 4 scarlet petals, the bases of which are black : the seed-vessel is roundish and smooth : common in corn-fields, flowering in summer. *P. Argemone,* the *Prickly-headed Poppy,* is also fairly common : it has smaller, paler flowers, and long seed-vessels, covered with stiff hairs.

117. Poppy, Corn-Rose.

118. Purple Clover, *Trifolium pratense,* Vetch family. The stem is prostrate at the base, and then rises to a height of about 1 ft., bearing dense, oval heads of many deep crimson, almost purple flowers : the leaves are compound, with 3 oval leaflets, and are provided with stipules : common in fields and pastures, and very frequently cultivated as a fodder plant : flowers throughout summer.

119. Marsh Cinquefoil, *Potentilla palustris,* Rose family. A common marsh plant : the stem rises

74

from the water : the leaves are feather-compound with 5 to 7 elliptical, serrate leaflets, and have stipules : the flowers are large, occurring in small groups at the tip of the stem, and are deep crimson brown, or with a purple tinge, in colour : flowers in August.

120. **Scarlet Pimpernel, Poor Man's Weather-Glass,** *Anagallis arvensis,* Primrose family. The

118. Purple Clover.

119. Marsh Cinquefoil.

stem is branched, lying along the ground, and rising at the tips : the leaves are in pairs, sessile, and ovate in shape : the flowers arise singly on slender stalks from the leaf axils ; they are small, star-like, and bright scarlet : a weed of dry, sandy soil, flowering in summer : this pretty little plant owes its second English name to the fact that the flowers close up in damp weather.

121. **Sheep's Sorrel,** *Rumex Acetosella,* Dock family. A weed, the occurrence of which in abun-

dance is a sure indication of poor soil : it is readily
recognised by its leaves, which are smooth, bright
green, and halbert-shaped ; the flowers are small
and inconspicuous, but gathered in a branched

120. Scarlet Pimpernel, Poor
Man's Weather-Glass.

121. Sheep's Sorrel.

spike at the end of the stem (9 ins. high) they make
a bright show of crimson variegated with green.
R. Acetosa, the *Sorrel,* or *Sourock,* has arrow-shaped
leaves of a pleasant acid flavour much appreciated
by children.

PALE PURPLE FLOWERS,

122–138.

A. Leaves compound, deeply cut, or lobed .   122–126

B. Leaves quite simple, at most toothed ' .   127–138

122. Cuckoo-Flower, Lady's Smock, *Cardamine pratensis*, Cress family. A conspicuous spring flower, of moist meadows : the stem is 1 to 1½ ft. high, and is crowned by a loose bunch of large lilac flowers :

122. Cuckoo-Flower, Lady's
Smock.

123. Sea-Rocket.

the leaves are feather-compound : the leaflets **of** the lower leaves are roundish; of the upper, lance-shaped : as the English name indicates, it flowers when the call of the cuckoo is heard.

123. Sea-Rocket, *Cakile maritima,* **Cress family.**

77

A curious little plant found on sandy sea-shores quite close to the high-water mark : the stem, which is usually less than 1 ft. high, is branched, and at the apex of each branch is a spike of fairly large, pale purple flowers : the leaves are cut deeply into lobes, and, as is often the case in seaside plants,

124. Stork's-bill.   125. Valerian.

are fat and fleshy : the fruit is a little pod, jointed in the middle ; when it is ripe the top joint falls off : flowers in summer.

124. **Stork's-bill**, *Erodium cicutarium*, Crane's-bill family. The stem lies along the sandy ground, on which the plant usually grows, and produces pairs of feather-compound leaves : the leaflets are in turn deeply cut into notched segments : the flower-stalks bear little umbels of pale purple flowers : the beaks of the ripe fruits show peculiar twisting movements when drying up, and help to scatter the seeds : flowers in summer and autumn.

125. Valerian, *Valeriana officinalis,* Valerian family. A handsome plant of stream sides and other damp places : it is readily picked out, even when not in flower, by the appearance of the leaves : they are feather-compound, with lance-shaped serrate leaflets, and in colour a curious greyish green, with a tinge of pink : the pale purple flowers are produced in large umbels at the end of the tall (2 to 4 ft.) stem, in summer : the seeds have little hairy floats.

126. Field Scabious, *Scabiosa arvensis,* Scabious

126. Field Scabious.   127. Marsh Violet.

family. A tall (2 to 3 ft.) plant of the fields and hedges, flowering in late summer : the leaves are lance-shaped and deeply notched, the upper more so than the lower : the flowers are gathered in large, pale purple, composite heads.

127. Marsh Violet, *Viola palustris,* Violet family. In marshes, in spring, may be found the small, pale purple flowers of this little plant : the petals are streaked with lines of darker colour : the leaves are rounded heart-shaped.

128. Willow Herb, *Epilobium montanum,* Willow herb family. The stem is generally about 1 ft. high :

it bears pairs of smooth, broad, lance-shaped, serrate
leaves, with quite short stalks : at the apex is a spike
of small pale purple flowers with 4 petals, and appar-
ently situated on long stalks, which are in reality
the seed-vessels : when ripe these open and set free
dozens of tiny seeds, each with a little hairy float,
by means of which they may be blown to a considerable distance by the
wind : the plant is common
but inconspicuous, in shady
places, where it flowers in
summer : it has several close

128. Willow Herb.   129. Marsh Pennywort.

relations, some of which prefer stream sides, and
which differ from it in the shape of the leaves and
other minor points.

129. **Marsh Pennywort,** *Hydrocotyle vulgaris,*
Hemlock family. This member of the hemlock
family is strikingly different from all those described
under " white " flowers : it is found in marshy
places, and has a slender creeping stem : at regular
intervals this sends a little bunch of roots into the
soil, and 2 to 5 leaves up to the air : the leaves have
long stalks joined to the middle of the lower surface,
and are circular : amongst the leaves are produced

in summer little stalked heads of pale purple flowers.

130. Field Madder, *Sherardia arvensis,* Bed-straw family. A pretty little plant of dry fields, flowering in summer : the stem is lowly, and much branched : the leaves are lance-shaped, pointed, and occur in whorls of 6 : at the tips of the branches are little groups of small, starry, lilac flowers.

130. Field Madder.   131. Butterbur.

131. Butterbur, *Petasites officinalis,* Daisy family. In April the *Butterbur* sends up a thick flower-stalk, with a large handsome spike of purplish flower-heads : only when these are fading do the leaves appear ; they are rounded, heart-shaped, with scalloped edges, and, when they have attained their full size, may measure a yard across ; the under surface is white with down : not uncommon along stream sides and on marshy ground.

132. Scottish Heather, Ling, *Calluna vulgaris,* Heath family. Familiar to all is this inhabitant of

the dry moors, which so transforms miles of mountain
country, when its pale purple flowers appear in late
summer : in size it varies from a little shrub a few
inches high to a large bush of 2 ft. or more : the

leaves are small, almost
scale-like, and arranged in
4 rows on the stem : the
flowers are in fine terminal
spikes ; the pure white
variety is quite rare, but
may be recognised even at
a distance by its paler,
bright green leaves.

133. Field Gentian, *Gen-
tiana campestris*, Gentian
family. A little plant of
dry heaths and grassy
places on the hills, flowering in autumn : the stem
is usually about 6 ins.
high, and often branched :
the leaves are in pairs,
smooth, and broadly lance-

132. Scottish Heather, Ling.   shaped : the flowers are
fairly large, tubular, pale
lilac, and occur in groups at the tip of the stem.
G. Amarella, the *Felwort*, is distinguished by having
5 petals instead of 4. *G. Pneumonanthe* is a much
more beautiful English plant, with large deep-blue
flowers.

134. Capitate Mint, *Mentha aquatica*, Dead-nettle
family. The stem is about 1½ to 2 ft. high, and
bears pairs of hairy, ovate, serrate leaves on short
stalks : in the axils of the uppermost leaves are
large, dense, globular clusters of small, pale purple
flowers, and the tip of the stem is occupied by a

similar cluster: the plant is common in damp
situations, flowering in late summer. *M. arvensis*,
the *Corn Mint*, is a smaller plant, common in corn-
fields, with the apical cluster wanting. *M. Pulegium*,
the *Pennyroyal*, is a prostrate, much branched plant,
with small leaves, and many clusters of flowers.
The mints are all fragrant.

135. Hemp-Nettle, *Galeopsis Tetrahit*, **Dead-nettle**

133. Field Gentian.   134. Capitate Mint.

family. A tall (1 to 2 ft.) coarse weed of cultivated land: the branched stem is square, and
bears pairs of ovate, serrate leaves with long
points: the flowers are small, with a 2-lipped,
pale purple corolla, and occur in little clusters
in the axils of the upper leaves, in late summer
and autumn.

136. Red Dead-Nettle, *Lamium purpureum*, **Dead-**
nettle family. One of the commonest weeds of gardens and cultivated land: the stem is branched,
spreading, and more or less prostrate: the leaves

are heart-shaped, with blunt serrations : the flowers,
which are pale reddish purple, occur in little clusters

135. Hemp-Nettle.   136. Red Dead-Nettle.

137. Spotted Hand-Orchis.   138. Scented Orchis.

in the axils of the leaves, and may be found practically
throughout the year.

137. Spotted Hand-Orchis, *Orchis maculata,* Orchis
family.   A common spring and early summer flower,
of moist woods and pastures ; the stem is $\frac{1}{2}$ to $1\frac{1}{2}$
ft. high, unbranched, and bears at its tip a thick
spike of pale purple flowers : these have short spurs
and large lips, which are generally spotted with
darker purple : the leaves are long, blunt, fleshy,
and spotted with dark brownish purple : if the plant
be dug up, it will be found to possess 2 fat tuberous
roots, besides several others more fibrous in character.

138. Scented Orchis, *Habenaria conopsea,* Orchis
family.   The stem is 9 to 12 ins. high, and bears a
spike of lilac-coloured flowers ; the flower has a long
delicate spur and a small lip : the leaves are long and
pointed : the flowers, which appear in early summer,
are very fragrant : common on moist heaths and
hilly roadsides.

PURPLE FLOWERS,
139–163.

A. Leaves compound, deeply cut, or lobed . **139–150**

B. Leaves quite simple, at most toothed . **151–163**

139. Heartsease, Pansy, *Viola tricolor,* Violet family. The stem is weak, and rambles in the coarse

grass of the pastures and wayside banks, where the plant commonly occurs : the leaves are ovate and bluntly serrate, but as they are provided with very large, deeply cut stipules, the effect is that of a much divided leaf : the flowers are large, and occur singly on long stalks in the leaf axils : the lower petal is spurred : the dominant colour of the flower is deep pure purple, but usually the 3 lower petals are paler, and one may be yellow : flowers from spring to autumn.

139. Heartsease, Pansy.

140. Bloody Crane's-bill, *Geranium sanguineum,* Crane's-bill family. A bushy plant, about 1 ft. high, not uncommon on dry cliffs and sandy banks, where it flowers in summer : the leaves are large, stalked, and deeply palm-cut into 7 notched segments : the

86

flowers occur singly on slender stalks in the leaf
axils ; they are large, brilliant red-purple, and very
handsome : the ripe fruits are scattered by the
peculiar movement of their beaks, which roll up like
watch-springs as they dry.

141. Field Crane's-bill, *Geranium pratense,* Crane's-
bill family.   The stem is tall (1 to 3 ft.) and much
branched : the leaves are large, sessile, and cut into

140. Bloody Crane's-bill.   141. Field Crane's-bill.

toothed lobes : the flowers are numerous, occur in
pairs, and are purple in colour : a common plant
of meadows and waysides, flowering in summer.

142. Herb Robert, *Geranium Robertianum,* Crane's-
bill family.   The weak, brittle stem is much branched,
and bears pairs of stalked leaves : the leaves are
compound, with 3 to 5 notched leaflets : the flowers,
which occur in pairs on slender stalks, are small
and reddish purple in colour : the whole plant is

sticky and resinous, and has a not unpleasant
odour : very common in damp shady places, flowering
from spring to autumn.

143. Tufted Vetch, *Vicia Cracca,* Vetch family.
A common and striking plant of dry banks and hedgerows : the long weak stem rambles over other plants,
aided by the slender-branched tendrils, which occupy
the tips of the leaves : the leaves are feather-com-

142. Herb Robert.   143. Tufted Vetch.

pound, with stipules : the leaflets, of which there
are about 10 pairs, are lance-shaped, and provided
with minute sharp points : from the axils of the upper
leaves spring the long flower-stalks, each with a
dense tuft of many small, bright bluish-purple
flowers : flowers in summer.

144. Bush Vetch, *Vicia sepium,* Vetch family.
Another common plant of banks and hedges : the
stem is not so long as that of the *Tufted Vetch,* and
there are only a few flowers in the shortly stalked

tufts: the leaves have about 6 pairs of narrowly ovate leaflets, with sharp points, and are provided with stipules and tendrils: the flowers, which are dull purple (rarely white), appear in summer.

145. **Tuberous Vetchling,** *Lathyrus montanus,* Vetch family. The stem is slender and prostrate: the leaves have 2 or 3 pairs of narrow elliptical leaflets, are provided with stipules, but are without tendrils, the tip of the leaf being occupied by a short

144. Bush Vetch.   145. Tuberous Vetchling.

point: the flower-stalks, arising in the axils of the leaves, are long and slender, with 3 or 4 flowers: the flowers are rich or sometimes pale purple in colour and appear in summer: the plant has a tuberous root, and is common in heathy woods and pastures and on moors.

146. **Hemp-Agrimony,** *Eupatorium cannabinum,* Daisy family. An ancient " simple," this fine plant grows in moist places along stream sides: the stem is 1 to 3 ft. high, with pairs of leaves so deeply cut

as to be almost compound : the lobes are 3 to 5 in number, and are serrate : the small flower-heads are massed in a large, flat inflorescence of a dull purple colour : flowers in late summer and autumn.

146. Hemp-Agrimony.   147. Spear Thistle.

147. Spear Thistle, *Cnic .s lanceolatus*, Daisy family. The national flower of Scotland is only too common in pastures and waste ground : it owes its wide distribution to the fact that the numerous little fruits are each provided with a very efficient float—the pappus—by means of which the wind can scatter them far and wide : the tall stem is clothed with oblong, jagged, and spiny leaves, and bears several large heads of purple flowers : flowers in late summer and autumn.

148. Marsh Thistle, *Cnicus palustris*, Daisy family. A less conspicuous plant than the *Spear Thistle*, but very common in damp places : the stem

may be over 3 ft. high, and is clothed with long,
deeply cut, and very spiny, dark green leaves : the
flower-heads are of medium size, occurring in clusters :
flowers purple, appearing in late summer. *C. arvensis*, the *Creeping Thistle*, which is similar, but with
whitish green leaves and paler flowers, is common on
waste ground.

149. **Knapweed**, *Centaurea nigra*, Daisy family.
A common plant in pastures, flowering from June
to autumn : the leaves are long, lance-shaped, and
the lower ones are deeply notched : the stem is 1 to
2 ft. high, and bears several large heads of deep
purple flowers.

150. **Bittersweet**, *Solanum Dulcamara*, Bittersweet family. The slender stem rambles amongst
bushes in hedges and woods : the leaves are almost

148. Marsh Thistle.   149. Knapweed.

compound, with 3 ovate lobes : the flowers occur in
drooping clusters, and resemble those of its relative
the potato in shape : the 5 petals are fine purple,

each with 2 green spots, and in the centre of the flower is a little yellow crown of stamens : the flowers appear in summer, and are followed by small, red, slightly poisonous berries : the plant was formerly much employed medicinally.

151. Sweet Violet, *Viola odorata*, Violet family. Less common than the *Dog Violet*, the *Sweet Violet* is found in hedgerows : the leaves are heart-shaped, with rounded tips and serrate margins : the flowers

150. Bittersweet.   151. Sweet Violet.

are purple in colour, or sometimes white, and sweet scented, appearing in spring : like the other violets, the sweet violet produces, besides the conspicuous coloured flowers, and later than these, small, green, bud-like flowers, which never open, but which nevertheless set abundant seed.

152. Dog Violet, *Viola canina*, Violet family. One of the commonest and prettiest of our wild flowers : it is found in woods, hedges, on banks, river shingle, and along stream sides : the leaves are in a tuft, and are heart-shaped, with serrate edges : the

flowers, borne singly on long stalks, are large, scentless, and purple, in some forms almost blue : one
petal is provided with a nec-
tar-containing spur : flowers
in spring and early summer.

    153. Red Campion, *Lychnis
dioica,* Chickweed family. A
handsome plant of hedges,
banks, and woods : the tall
(2 ft.) stem bears pairs of
downy ovate leaves : the
flowers, crowded at the apex,
are large and red purple :
male and female flowers occur

152. Dog Violet.

on different plants. *L. alba* is a very similar plant,

153. Red Campion.

154. Corn-Cockle.

with white flowers, which have a delicate scent in
the evening ; both flower in summer.

    154. Corn - Cockle, *Lychnis Githago,* Chickweed

family. A striking weed of corn-fields : the stem
is about 2 ft. high, with pairs of lance-shaped leaves :
the flowers occur singly on stalks in the axils of the
upper leaves ; they are large and bright purple : if
abundant, it is dangerous, as the seeds are poisonous
and contaminate the grain with which they become
mixed : flowers in summer.

155. **Fine-leaved Heath,** *Erica cinerea,* Heath

155. Fine-leaved Heath.　　　156. Foxglove.

family. A small plant of dry heaths : the stem is
erect, branched, and about 4 to 6 ins. high : the
leaves are in whorls, generally of 3 : the flowers,
which occur in little clusters at the tips of the
branches, are small, egg-shaped, with the mouth of
the corolla pointing downwards and outwards ;
they are a rich purple in colour, and appear in
summer.

156. **Foxglove,** *Digitalis purpurea,* Foxglove family. One of our most beautiful woodland plants :

it produces in the first year a rosette of soft, broad, lance-shaped leaves, with serrate edges, and from this arise, in succeeding years, the tall, flowering stems : the flowers, which open in summer, are arranged in a handsome terminal spike : they are large, pendant, purple or rarely white, and, as the English and Latin names suggest, in shape like the finger of a glove : one of the few native plants which is still used medicinally, it contains a strong poisonous essence.

157. Butterwort.   158. Wild Thyme.

157. Butterwort, *Pinguicula vulgaris,* Butterwort family. A pretty little plant of bogs and wet heaths : the leaves, which are grouped in a rosette, are broadly elliptical, bright green, and viscid : from the rosette rise several slender flowering-stalks, each with a single flower, which superficially resembles that of the violet, and which is violet in colour : the edges of the leaves roll in on any insect which lights on them, and the prey is digested and utilised as food : flowers in early summer.

158. Wild Thyme, *Thymus Serpyllum,* Dead-nettle family. The stem is more or less woody, much branched, and spreads itself out on the dry banks, where the plant grows : the leaves are in pairs, small, and lance-shaped : the flowers are gathered at the tips of short, erect branches ; they are small, purple, and appear in summer : the whole plant is pleasantly aromatic.

159. Ground-Ivy, *Nepeta Glechoma,* Dead-nettle family. The stem is branched and prostrate, with pairs of rounded, heart-shaped leaves on long stalks : the leaf margins are scalloped : the flowers are in clusters in the axils of the upper leaves : the corolla protrudes markedly from the calyx, and is bright blue-purple : common in shady woods, flowering in spring and early summer.

160. Self-heal, *Prunella vulgaris,* Dead-nettle family. A very common plant of meadows and pas-

159. Ground-Ivy.   **160. Self-heal.**

tures, flowering in summer : the stem is less than 1 ft. long, and has pairs of blunt, ovate leaves : the flowers are crowded into terminal heads of a dull

purple colour : occasionally white-flowered plants
are found : formerly a highly prized " simple."

161. Betony, *Stachys Betonica*, Dead-nettle family.

161. Betony.   162. Hedge-Woundwort.

A plant of the woods and hedges : it may be most
readily recognised by its paired, stalked leaves,
which are oblong, with the base heart-shaped, and
with bluntly serrate margins : the stem is 1 to 2 ft.
high, with the red-purple flowers mostly gathered
in short terminal spikes : flowers in late summer and
autumn.

162. Hedge-Woundwort, *Stachys sylvatica*, Dead-
nettle family. A common plant of woods and
thickets : the tall rank stem has pairs of large,
stalked, serrate, heart-shaped leaves, with a peculiar
soft, hairy surface : the flowers, which are small
and dull purple, occur in little groups in the axils
of the upper leaves : the plant has an unpleasant
fœtid odour, and was formerly used as a salve for cuts.

163. Early Purple Orchis.

163. **Early Purple Orchis,** *Orchis mascula,* Orchis family. A fairly common and very handsome plant of pastures, flowering in early summer : the stem is 1 ft. high, and bears a long loose spike of fine purple flowers, each with a spur and a broad 3-lobed lip, the middle lobe notched in the middle : the leaves are long, fleshy, and spotted. *O. latifolia,* the *Marsh Orchis,* has a denser spike, of deep purple flowers, the lips of which are only very slightly lobed : it is common on moist pastures, flowering in summer.

BLUE FLOWERS,
164–177.

164. Milkwort, *Polygala vulgaris,* Milkwort family.
A little plant of pastures and heaths, remarkable
for the colour variations of its flowers : the most

164. Milkwort.   165. Devil's-bit Scabious.

common colour is deep blue, but pink, white, and
sky-blue are very frequent : the stem is branched
at the base ; each branch is about 4 ins. high, with
small lance-shaped leaves, and a spike of flat flowers :
flowers in summer.

165. Devil's-bit Scabious, *Scabiosa Succisa,* Sca-

bious family. The stem is usually unbranched and
about 2 ft. high: there is a tuft of leaves at the
base and a few pairs on the stem, oblong-elliptical,
and sometimes slightly notched : the flowers are
gathered in small, round heads, blue, with a slight
tinge of purple, occasionally white : the name refers
to the character of the underground stock, which

166. Sea Starwort.   167. Corn-flower, Bluebottle.

ends abruptly, as if bitten off : a common plant of
dry pastures, flowering in late summer and autumn.

166. Sea Starwort, *Aster Tripolium*, Daisy family.
A plant of salt-marshes near the sea : the stem
is 1 to 2 ft. high, with long, elliptical leaves,
which are usually somewhat fleshy : the flowers
are in large handsome heads, with a bright blue ray
and yellow disc : flowers in autumn.

167. Corn-flower, Bluebottle, *Centaurea Cyanus*,
Daisy family. One of the most beautiful plants
of our corn-fields, flowering in late summer : the
stem is tall and slender, with many narrow leaves :

the flowers are in heads, those at the margin of the
head being large and bright blue, those at the centre
smaller and more purple.

168. Chicory, Succory, *Cichorium Intybus*, Daisy
family. The stem is about 2 ft. high: the lower
leaves are oblong in shape, with broad toothed segments: the upper leaves are smaller, toothed, lance-

168. Chicory, Succory.   169. Giant Bell-flower.

shaped, and clasp the stem: the flower-heads are
large and of a fine blue colour; usually only a few
are open at one time, and these are then surmounted
by spikes of buds: not uncommon on waste ground,
flowering in late summer and autumn.

169. Giant Bell-flower, *Campanula latifolia*, Hairbell family. A tall, handsome plant of shady
places, flowering in late summer and autumn: the
leaves are stalked, narrowly ovate in shape, and with
serrate margins: the flowers, which are gathered
in a long terminal spike, are large, bell-shaped, erect,
and of a fine blue colour.

170. Hairbell, *Campanula rotundifolia,* Hairbell family. The *Bluebell of Scotland* is one of the most familiar flowers of dry pastures and banks : the

170. Hairbell. 171. Bugloss.

slender stem is about 1 ft. high, with many narrow leaves : the round leaves of the Latin name are found at the base of the stem, hidden by the grass in which the plant grows : the flowers, which occur in graceful spikes, are bright blue, or rarely white, bell-shaped, and pendant : the English name is also written *Harebell.*

171. Bugloss, *Lycopsis arvensis,* Forget-me-not family. An inconspicuous inhabitant of fields and waste ground : the stem is about 1 ft. high and slightly branched : the leaves are bluntly lance-shaped : both stem and leaves are very rough, with short stiff hairs : the small blue flowers are gathered in terminal spikes : flowers in summer.

172. Forget-me-not, *Myosotis·scorpioides,* Forget-me-not family. Several closely-related species of

Myosotis are common in this country, but the most beautiful is *M. scorpioides*, which is found in ditches : the leaves are elliptical, and bright green : the flowers, which are larger than those of any other common native species, have a salver-shaped, bright blue corolla, with a yellow eye : they occur in spikes at the apex of the stem : flowers in summer and autumn.

173. Variegated Forget-me-not, *Myosotis versicolor,* Forget-me-not family. A common plant of fields and waste places : the stem is slender, slightly branched, about $\frac{1}{2}$ to $1\frac{1}{2}$ ft. high : the leaves, which are mostly gathered at the base, are elliptical : the flowers occur in slender spikes, are quite small, and when nearly open are yellow, changing to pink, and finally to blue : flowers in early summer.

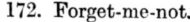

172. Forget-me-not.

173. Variegated Forget-me-not.

174. Viper's Bugloss, *Echium vulgare,* Forget-me-not family. The stem is very rough with stiff hairs, and reaches a height of 1 to 2 ft. : the leaves,

which are also rough, are lance-shaped and fairly
large : the flowers are massed in a handsome terminal spike : the corolla is tubular and twisted, at
first dull purple, but, when fully open, changing to a
deep blue : not uncommon on dry banks, flowering
in summer.

175. Germander Speedwell, *Veronica Chamœdrys,*
Foxglove family. A very pretty woodland flower :
the stem is more or less prostrate, with pairs
of sessile, ovate, serrate leaves ; from the axils of
the upper leaves arise slender stalks, each with a
spike of large blue flowers : the corolla has 4 petals,
very unequal in size, the lower one being much
smaller than the others. A very different-looking
plant is the *Brooklime, V. Beccabunga,* which is
common in ditches : the stem is thick, with pairs of

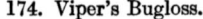

174. Viper's Bugloss.   175. Germander Speedwell.

smooth, fleshy leaves : the little spikes of flowers
resemble those of the *Speedwell,* though the flowers
are smaller.

176. Bugle, *Ajuga reptans,* Dead-nettle family.
A common early summer plant of damp meadows
and stream sides : from the base of the stem arise

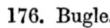

176. Bugle.

177. Wood Hyacinth, English
Bluebell.

several prostrate runners, which, like it, bear pairs
of smooth, oval leaves : the flowering stem is erect,
about 6 ins. high, with little groups of flowers in the
axils of the upper leaves : the corolla is tubular, with
a large, lobed lower lip ; the upper lip, which is
present in most members of this family, is wanting :
flowers blue, occasionally white.

177. Wood Hyacinth, English Bluebell, *Scilla
non-scripta,* Hyacinth family. The plant rests in
the form of a bulb throughout the winter, and in
spring sends up several long, narrow, fleshy leaves :
in early summer appears the flower-stalk, about
9 ins. high, with a terminal spike of drooping, bell-
shaped flowers, bright blue in colour : a flower of
woods and hedgerows.

BROWN FLOWERS,
178–184.

178. Hare's-foot Trefoil, *Trifolium arvense*, Vetch family. On dunes and other sandy ground the *Hare's-foot Trefoil* is frequently met with : the stem is branched, often creeping, and may reach a length

178. Hare's-foot Trefoil.   179. Cudweed.

of about 1 ft. : the leaves are compound, with 3 narrow leaflets : the flowers are united in stalked, oval heads, of a light greyish-brown colour : flowers in late summer and autumn.

179. Cudweed, *Gnaphalium sylvaticum*, Daisy family. A common, but not very conspicuous, plant of dry fields and pastures, flowering in late summer : the simple stem is usually 6 to 9 ins. high, but varies greatly, and may be much taller or shorter : the small, oval flower-heads are chocolate-brown in colour, and form a spike on the upper half of the stem : the leaves are narrowly lance-shaped. The *Marsh Cudweed*, a related plant of moist meadows, has a shorter, branched stem and paler flower-heads.

180. Knotted Figwort.   181. Ribwort.

180. Knotted Figwort, *Scrophularia nodosa*, **Fox-**glove family.   The tall (2 to 4 ft.) stem is markedly square, and bears pairs of large, ovate, serrate leaves ; it is thickened at the points where these arise : the flowers are small, roundish, and rich brown and green in colour : common in moist shady places, flowering in summer.

181. Ribwort, *Plantago lanceolata*, Plantain family. A familiar weed of road-sides and grassy places : from the rosette of long, ribbed, lance-shaped leaves spring

several flower-stalks, from 3 ins. to 1 ft. high : each
bears a single head of small flowers, which is dark
brown or black in colour, except when the flowers
are fully open, when it takes on a greyish or yellowish
tinge : the *Carl-Doddie* of Scottish children, from its
use in an ancient war-game of *Charles* against *George :*
flowers in summer.

182. **Common Rush,** *Juncus communis,* Rush

 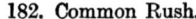 

182. Common Rush.   183. Great Wood-Rush.

family.   The short creeping stock gives rise to long,
slender, cylindrical, green stems about 2 ft. high and
sharply pointed : at the base of these are 2 or 3
sheaths, which represent the leaves : the stems are
soft, and filled with a white pith, which is used even
to-day as a lamp-wick : some of the stems are
barren, but from near the apex of others springs a
dense, **round** head of brown flowers : flowers in
summer **on** marshy ground.

183. **Great Wood-Rush,** *Luzula sylvatica,* Rush

family. A very common plant in shady woods, where it often covers large patches of soil : the leaves, which arise in tufts, are sword-shaped, and dark, shining green, the edges covered with long, silky hairs : the flowers are small, pale brown, and occur in a branched cluster, at the apex of the flowering stem : flowers in spring and early summer.

184. Reed - Mace, *Typha latifolia,* Reed-mace family. A typical plant of the margins of ponds and lakes : the stem may be 6 ft. high, and bears at its tip 2 inflorescences : the lower is firm, cylindrical, dark brown, and consists

184. Reed-Mace.

of female flowers ; the upper is looser, paler, and consists of male flowers : the leaves are broad and long, overtopping the inflorescences : a species with narrower and shorter leaves is also found : flowers in summer.

GREEN FLOWERS,

185–195.

185. Lady's Mantle, *Alchemilla vulgaris,* Rose
family. A common plant of moist pastures, flowering in summer : it is readily recognised by its leaves,

185. Lady's Mantle. 186. Golden Saxifrage.

which are almost round and palm-lobed, with about
7 serrate lobes : they are unwettable, and when
plunged in water or covered with rain-drops take
on a silvery appearance : they are provided with
stipules, and when young are plaited : the flowers
are small, star-like, yellowish green, and occur in
brushes at the end of the flowering stems.

186. Golden Saxifrage, *Chrysosplenium oppositi-*

folium, Saxifrage family. A spring flowering plant of stream sides and wet places, particularly in woods : the stem may be 6 ins. high, with pairs of shortly stalked, roundish leaves with scalloped edges : the flowers are small, in numerous little groups at the apex of the stem, and are green with a golden tinge.

187. Moschatel, *Adoxa Moschatellina*, Moschatel

187. Moschatel.   188. Goose-foot, Fat Hen.

family. A delicate little plant of damp woods, flowering in spring : the stem is horizontal, and lies just under the surface of the soil : it sends up several stalked leaves, and a single flower-stalk with 2 leaves, and a little head of 5 flowers : the leaves are compound, with 3 leaflets, each 3-lobed : the flowers are pale green : the apical flower of the head has 4 petals, and the others have each 5.

188. Goose-foot, Fat Hen, *Chenopodium album*, Goose-foot family. A common weed of waste ground and cultivated land, flowering in autumn : the stem is tall and branched, with stalked rhomboid-shaped leaves, the margins of which are coarsely toothed : the flowers are small and greenish, in little spikes in the axils of the upper leaves : the plant has a slightly mealy appearance.

189. Black Bindweed, *Polygonum Convolvulus,* Dock family. A common and troublesome weed of gardens : the root descends to great depths, and is very difficult to eradicate : in corn-fields it twines round the stems of the corn : the leaves are arrow-shaped, and in their axils occur in summer and autumn little spikes of green flowers, tinged with pink.

190. Curled Dock, *Rumex crispus,* Dock family.

189. Black Bindweed.   190. Curled Dock.

The stem is about 3 ft. high, and bears very large, long, lance-shaped, wavy leaves : the flowers are small, green, pendulous, and occur in prominent, branched, terminal spikes : the stem and flowers have often a reddish tinge : there are several closely-related species, which differ only in details : common

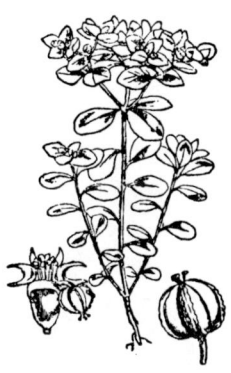 

191. Petty Spurge.　　　192. Dog's Mercury.

about cultivated land, flowering in summer and autumn.

191. **Petty Spurge,** *Euphorbia Peplus,* Spurge family. The *Spurges* are readily recognised among our green-flowered plants by the fact that they exude a milky juice when wounded : the stem is branched, with smooth leaves of a fine green, oval or ovate in shape : the apparent flowers are small and green ; in reality they are little inflorescences of much-simplified flowers : a common garden weed, flowering in autumn : the *Sun Spurge* is a common field weed, with serrate leaves and yellowish green inflorescences.

192. **Dog's Mercury,** *Mercurialis perennis,* Spurge family. A common spring plant of shady woods :

(2,050)　　　　　　　　　　　　　8

the stem is about 1 ft. high, with pairs of broadly
lance-shaped, serrate leaves : the flowers are of
two kinds, male and female, occurring on different
plants : they are in little spikes in the axils of the
upper leaves, the former yellowish green, the latter
green : highly poisonous.

193. Bur-reed, *Sparganium erectum,* Bur-reed
family. A common plant growing in the muddy

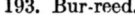

193. Bur-reed.   194. Cuckoo-Pint, Lords-
                              and-Ladies.

margins of sluggish streams : the stem is about
2 ft. high, and is slightly branched : the flowers are
gathered into spiky, spherical, green heads, which
are situated about the tips of the branches : the
leaves are long and sword-shaped : flowers in
summer.

194. Cuckoo-Pint, Lords-and-Ladies, *Arum macu-*
latum, Cuckoo-pint family. The plant at once attracts
attention by its large, glossy, arrow-shaped leaves,

which rise from the ground on longish stalks : among them appear in April or May the curious inflorescences : these consist of a stalk, on which are arranged first female flowers reduced to a single seed-vessel, then male flowers reduced to a single stamen, above these a circle of stout hairs, and finally a long, dark purple club, the whole being enclosed by a long, pointed, pale-green hood : in autumn the hood and the upper parts of the inflorescence die away, leaving the stalk crowned by a little bunch of scarlet berries : not uncommon in woods and hedges.

195. Cotton-Grass, *Eriophorum polystachion*, Sedge family. A striking plant of boggy ground : the leaves are long, narrow, and pointed : the stem is slender, about 1 ft. high, and bears several heads of flowers on delicate drooping flower-stalks : in colour they are greenish, tinged with yellow and brown : the plant is most remarkable when in fruit, as the head then presents the appearance

195. Cotton-Grass.

of a flock of cotton-wool. *Hare's-tail Cotton-grass*, a related species, bears only a single, erect flower-head on each stalk : flowers in summer.

FLOWERS RARELY FOUND OR VERY INCONSPICUOUS, 196–200.

196. Mare's-Tail, *Hippuris vulgaris,* Mare's-tail family. A not uncommon plant of quiet water : the stem is partly (or in running water completely)

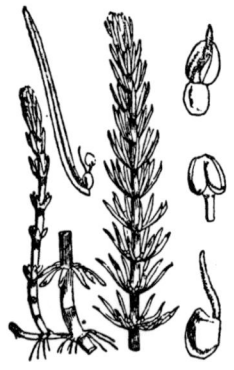 

196. Mare's-Tail.   197. Water-Milfoil.

submerged : it is simple or slightly branched, with many whorls, of 6 to 12 stiff, narrow leaves, with hard points : the submerged leaves are soft and

116

long : flowers very small, in the axils of the upper leaves, in summer.

197. Water-Milfoil, *Myriophyllum spicatum,* Mare's-tail family. A common plant of ponds and slow streams : the slender stem bears whorls of 4 brownish, feather-like leaves : the plant is submerged, except for the slender terminal spikes of very small flowers, which appear in summer.

198. Water-Starwort.

198. Water-Starwort, *Callitriche aquatica,* Mare's-tail family. An extremely common plant of ditches, ponds, and quiet streams : the stem is slender, branched, and has pairs of elliptical leaves, broader towards the tip : in some forms the leaves are quite narrow and pointed : flowers small, and green in the leaf axils : the plant is of a fresh green colour.

199. Greater Bladderwort.

199. Greater Bladder-wort, *Utricularia vulgaris,* Butterwort family. A fairly common submerged plant of pools, especially on peaty soil : the leaves are very much divided into narrow, hair-like segments ; some of the segments are replaced by little bladders, which act as traps for small water-animals, the dead bodies of which are utilised by the plant as food : the large yellow flowers are produced in spikes above the water in summer, but the plant flowers only rarely.   The *Lesser Bladderwort* has more slender leaves and small pale flowers.

200. Water-Thyme.

200. Water-Thyme, *Elodea canadensis*, Water-thyme family.   The stems are long, slender, and submerged, with close whorls of 3 narrow, blunt, olive-green leaves : the flowers, which are rarely seen, are small, on slender stalks, and pale violet.   The plant is not a native, but since its introduction from America it has spread enormously, and often seriously chokes ponds and canals.

INDEX OF LATIN NAMES.

The numbers refer to the figure numbers, not to the pages.

ACHILLEA, 2, 3.
Adoxa, 187.
Ægopodium, 7.
Agrimonia, 80.
Ajuga, 176.
Alchemilla, 185.
Alisma, 115.
Allium, 42.
Anagallis, 120.
Anemone, 17.
Angelica, 13.
Antennaria, 107.
Anthriscus, 12.
Anthyllis, 74.
Arum, 194.
Asperula, 29.
Aster, 166.

BARBAREA, 68.
Bellis, 1.
Brassica, 69.
Butomus, 116.

CAKILE, 123.
Callitriche, 198.
Calluna, 132.
Caltha, 93.
Campanula, 169, 170.
Capsella, 22.
Cardamine, 21, 122.
Castalia, 44.
Caucalis, 15.

Centaurea, 149, 167.
Cerastium, 43.
Chelidonium, 67.
Chenopodium, 188.
Chrysanthemum, 4, 52.
Chrysosplenium, 186.
Cichorium, 168.
Clematis, 16.
Cnicus, 147, 148.
Cochlearia, 34.
Conium, 6.
Conopodium, 9.
Convolvulus, 111.
Corydalis, 19.
Crepis, 58.

DIANTHUS, 105.
Digitalis, 156.
Drosera, 39.

ECHIUM, 174.
Elodea, 200.
Epilobium, 128.
Erica, 108, 155.
Eriophorum, 195.
Erodium, 124.
Erophila, 33.
Erythræa, 110.
Eupatorium, 146.
Euphorbia, 191.
Euphrasia, 31.

Fumaria, 100.

Galeopsis, 86, 135.
Galium, 26, 27, 28, 81, 82.
Genista, 97.
Gentiana, 133.
Geranium, 140, 141, 142.
Geum, 77, 102.
Gnaphalium, 179.

Habenaria, 138.
Helianthemum, 95.
Heracleum, 14.
Hieracium, 59, 60.
Hippuris, 196.
Hydrocotyle, 129.
Hypericum, 96.
Hypochæris, 61.

Juncus, 182.

Lamium, 136.
Lapsana, 57.
Lathyrus, 76, 145.
Leontodon, 62.
Lepidium, 36.
Linaria, 83.
Lotus, 75.
Luzula, 183.
Lychnis, 106, 153, 154.
Lycopsis, 171.
Lysimachia, 88, 89.

Matricaria, 5.
Medicago, 71.
Melilotus, 72.
Mentha, 134.
Menyanthes, 103.
Mercurialis, 192.
Mimulus, 84.
Myosotis, 172, 173.
Myriophyllum, 197.
Myrrhis, 10.

Narthecium, 90.
Nasturtium, 20.
Nepeta, 159.
Nymphæa, 94.

Ononis, 101.
Orchis, 137, 163.
Oxalis, 23.

Papaver, 17.
Parnassia, 38.
Pedicularis, 104.
Petasites, 131.
Pimpinella, 8.
Pinguicula, 157.
Plantago, 181.
Polygala, 164.
Polygonum, 112, 113, 114, 189.
Potentilla, 78, 79, 119.
Primula, 87.
Prunella, 160.
Pyrola, 49.

Ranunculus, 18, 66, 91, 92.
Reseda, 70.
Rhinanthus, 85.
Rumex, 121, 190.

Sagina, 47.
Sagittaria, 50.
Scabiosa, 126, 168.
Scandix, 11.
Scilla, 177.
Scrophularia, 180.
Sedum, 99.
Senecio, 55, 56.
Sherardia, 130.
Sisymbrium, 35.
Solanum, 150.
Solidago, 51.
Sonchus, 64.
Sparganium, 193.
Spergula, 48.

Spiræa, 25.
Stachys, 161, 162.
Statice, 109.
Stellaria, 45, 46.
Symphytum, 41.

TANACETUM, 53.
Taraxacum, 63.
Teucrium, 32.
Thlaspi, 37.
Thymus, 158.
Tragopogon, 65.

Trientalis, 40.
Trifolium, 24, 73, 118, 178.
Tussilago, 54.
Typha, 184.

ULEX, 98.
Utricularia, 199.

VALERIANA, 125.
Veronica, 30, 175.
Vicia, 143, 144.
Viola, 127, 139, 151, 152.

INDEX OF ENGLISH NAMES.

The numbers refer to the figure numbers, not to the pages.

AGRIMONY, 80.
Anemone, 17.
Angelica, 13.
Arrow-head, 50.
Avens, 102.

BED-STRAW, 26, 27, 82.
Bell-flower, 169.
Betony, 161.
Bindweed, 111, 230.
Bird's-foot Trefoil, 75.
Bishop's-weed, 7.
Bitter-Cress, 21.
Bittersweet, 150.
Black Bindweed, 189.
Bladderwort, 199.
Bluebell, 170, 177.
Blue-bottle, 167.
Bog-Asphodel, 90.
Brandy-bottle, 94.
Brooklime, 175.
Buckbean, 103.
Bugle, 176.
Bugloss, 171, 174.
Burnet-Saxifrage, 8.
Bur-reed, 193.
Butterbur, 131.
Buttercup, 66.
Butterwort, 157.

CAMPION, 153.
Cat's-ear, 61.
Cat's-foot, 107.
Celandine, 67, 92.

Centaury, 110.
Chamomile, 5.
Charlock, 69.
Chervil, 12.
Chickweed, 45.
Chickweed Wintergreen, 40.
Chicory, 168.
Cleavers, 28.
Clover, 24, 118.
Coltsfoot, 54.
Comfrey, 41.
Corn-Cockle, 154.
Corn-flower, 167.
Corn-Marigold, 52.
Corn-Rose, 117.
Cotton-grass, 195.
Cow-parsnip, 14.
Cowslip, 87.
Crane's-bill, 140, 141.
Crosswort, 81.
Crowfoot, 18, 66.
Cuckoo-flower, 122.
Cuckoo-pint, 194.
Cudweed, 179.

DAISY, 1.
Dandelion, 63.
Dead-nettle, 136.
Devil's-bit, 165.
Dock, 190.
Dog's Mercury, 192.
Dutch Clover, 24.

EYEBRIGHT, 31.

122

FAT HEN, 188.
Felwort, 133.
Feverfew, 4.
Figwort, 180.
Flowering-rush, 116.
Forget-me-not, 172, 173.
Foxglove, 156.
Fumitory, 19, 100.
Furze, 98.

GARLIC, 42.
Gentian, 133.
Goat's-beard, 65.
Golden-rod, 51.
Golden Saxifrage, 186.
Goldilocks, 82.
Goosefoot, 190
Goose-grass, 28.
Gorse, 98.
Goutweed, 7.
Grass of Parnassus, 38.
Ground Ivy, 159.
Groundsel, 55.

HAIRBELL, 170.
Hare's-foot Trefoil, 178.
Hawkbit, 62.
Hawk's-beard, 58.
Hawkweed, 59, 60.
Heartsease, 139.
Heath, 108, 155.
Heather, 132.
Hedge Parsley, 15.
Hemlock, 6.
Hemp-Agrimony, 146.
Hemp-nettle, 86, 135.
Herb Robert, 142.
Hog-weed, 14.
Hyacinth, 177.

JACK-BY-THE-HEDGE, 35.
Jack-go-to-bed-at-Noon, 65.

KIDNEY VETCH, 74.
Knapweed, 149.
Knot-grass, 112.

LADY'S FINGER, 74.
Lady's Mantle, 185.
Lady's Smock, 122.
Ling, 132.
Loosestrife, 88.
Lords-and-Ladies, 194.
Louse-wort, 104.

MADDER, 130.
Maiden Pink, 105.
Mare's-tail, 196.
Marsh-Cinquefoil, 119.
Marsh-Marigold, 93.
Mayweed, 5.
Meadow-Sweet, 25.
Medick, 71.
Melilot, 72.
Mignonette, 70.
Milkwort, 164.
Millefoil, 2.
Mint, 134.
Moneywort, 89.
Moschatel, 187.
Mountain-Everlasting, 107.
Mouse-ear, 43.
Musk, 84.
Mustard, 87.
Myrrh, 10.

NIPPLEWORT, 57.

OLD MAN'S BEARD, 16.
Orchis, 137, 138, 163.
Ox-eye, 4.

PANSY, 139.
Pearlwort, 47.
Penny Cress, 37.
Pennyroyal, 164.
Pennywort, 129.
Pepperwort, 36.
Persicaria, 113, 114.
Petty Whin, 97.
Pig-nut, 9.
Pimpernel, 89, 120.

Pink, 105.
Plantain, 181.
Poor Man's Weather-glass, 120.
Poppy, 117.
Primrose, 87.

QUEEN - OF - THE - MEADOW, 25.

RAGGED ROBIN, 106.
Ragwort, 56.
Ramsons, 42.
Red-Rattle, 104.
Reed-mace, 184.
Rest-harrow, 101.
Ribwort, 181.
Rocket, 68.
Rock-rose, 95.
Rush, 182.

ST. JOHN'S WORT, 96.
Sauce-alone, 35.
Scabious, 126, 165.
Scurvy-grass, 34.
Sea-Daisy, 109.
Sea-Rocket, 123.
Self-heal, 160.
Shepherd's Needle, 11.
Silver-weed, 79.
Sneezewort, 3.
Sorrel, 121.
Sourock, 121.
Sowthistle, 64.
Spearwort, 91.
Speedwell, 30, 175.
Spurge, 191.
Spurrey, 48.
Starwort, 166.
Stitchwort, 46.
Stonecrop, 99.

Stork's-bill, 124.
Succory, 168.
Sundew, 39.
Sweet Cicely, 10.

TANSY, 53.
Thistle, 147, 148.
Thrift, 109.
Thyme, 158.
Toad-flax, 83.
Tormentil, 78.
Traveller's Joy, 16.
Trefoil, 73, 75, 178.

VALERIAN, 125.
Vetch, 143, 144.
Vetchling, 76, 145.
Violet, 127, 151, 152.
Viper's Bugloss, 174.

WALL-PEPPER, 99.
Water-Cress, 20.
Water-Lily, 44, 94.
Water-Milfoil, 197.
Water-Plantain, 115.
Water-Starwort, 198.
Water-Thyme, 200.
Weld, 70.
Whin, 98.
Whitlow-grass, 33.
Willow Herb, 128.
Winter-green, 49.
Woodruff, 29.
Woodrush, 183.
Wood-Sage, 32.
Wood-Sorrel, 23.
Woundwort, 162.

YARROW, 2.
Yellow Rattle, 85.

PRINTED IN GREAT BRITAIN AT
THE PRESS OF THE PUBLISHERS.

Lightning Source UK Ltd.
Milton Keynes UK
UKOW051809230712

196444UK00001B/95/A